1 MONTH OF
FREE
READING

at

www.ForgottenBooks.com

By purchasing this book you are eligible for one month membership to ForgottenBooks.com, giving you unlimited access to our entire collection of over 700,000 titles via our web site and mobile apps.

To claim your free month visit:

www.forgottenbooks.com/free173943

ISBN 978-0-265-17936-9
PIBN 10173943

Union University Bulletin

Jackson, Tennessee

Catalogue
1923-1924

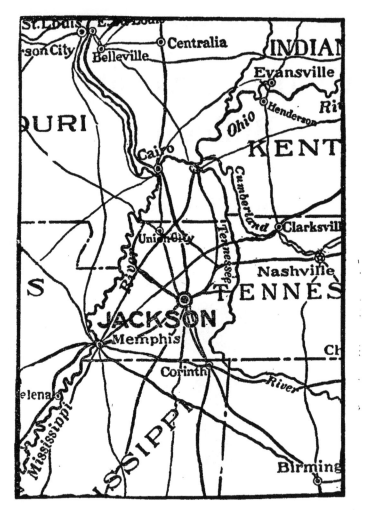

Union University is located at Jackson, Tennessee, a great railroad center. Note how accessible it is to all parts of the country.

Volume XVI   JUNE 1923   Number 1

Union University Bulletin
Jackson, Tennessee

CATALOG

Eighty-first Annual Session
1923-1924

Published Bi-monthly by Union University, Jackson, Tenn. Entered as Second Class Matter August 5, 1915, at Post Office, Jackson, Tenn.,
Under Act of Congress of August 24, 1912.

1923

Index

University Calendar

1923

September 17, Monday—
    Martriculation.

September 18, Tuesday—
    Matriculation and formal opening.

November 22, Thursday—
    Thanksgiving Holiday and Reception at Adams Hall.

December 21 to January 1—
    Christmas Holidays.

1924

January 1, Wednesday—
    Winter Term begins.

March 17, Monday—
    Spring Term begins.

Saturday, May 24, (night)—
    Contest for Eaton Medal.

Sunday, May 25, (morning)—
    Baccalaureate Sermon (First Baptist Church).

Sunday, May 25, (night)—
    J. R. Graves Annual Sermon.

Monday, May 26, (morning)—
    J. R. G. Society final meeting and contest for J. W. Porter Award.

Monday, May 26, (afternoon)—
    Rhodes Medal Contest.

Monday, May 26, (afternoon)—
    Annual Meeting of Board of Trustees.

Monday, May 26, (night)—
    Academy Graduation Exercises.

Tuesday, May 27, (morning)—
    Athletic Field Day.

Tuesday, May 27, (afternoon)—
    Alumni Reunion.

Tuesday, May 27, (night)—
    Alumni Banquet.

Wednesday, May 28, (morning)—
    University Graduation Exercises.

Board of Trustees

Faculty for 1923-24

GEORGE MARTIN SAVAGE, A. M., LL. D.
President Emeritus

J. R. Graves, Professor of Logic and French.
A. B. Union University, 1871; thirty-five years Professor in Union University, eighteen years President of Union University; traveled and studied in Europe and Asia eleven months, 1905-06.

HENRY EUGENE WATTERS, A. M., D. D., LL. D.
President
Chair of Sociology.

A. B. Union University, 1904; A. M. Union University, 1916; Graduate student Brown University, 1905-06; D. D., 1906; LL. D., Union University, 1921; seven years Principal in Public Schools; eleven years President of Hall-Moody Institute; President of College of Marshall, 1916-18; President of Union University 1918-

ARTHUR WARREN PRINCE, A. M.
Dean

A. B. William Jewell, 1904; A. M. William Jewell, 1905; Graduate student University of Chicago, 1907, 1914, 1920, 21; Principal Annapolis, Mo., 1901-02; Instructor in Physics, William Jewell, 1904-05; Head of Science Department Western Military Academy, Alton, Ill., 1905-08; Head of Science Department Union University, 1908-

L. R. HOGAN, A. M., D. D., Ph. D.
Chair of Education

A. B. graduate Mercer University; two years graduate work University of Chicago; one year graduate work Columbia University; studied one year in Union Theological Seminary; traveled and studied in Europe; Ph. D. with conditions; Principal of the Public Schools, Tiptonia, Ga.; Vice-President Locust Grove Institute; Professor in Bessie Tift College; Professor in Shorter College; Dean Meridian College; Head Department Education Union University, 1921.

CHAS. W. DAVIS, M. S., Ph. D.
Biology and Agriculture.

B. S. University of Tennessee; M. S. and Ph. D., Iowa State Agricultural College; Principal of Academy in Georgia; Head of Agricultural Department West Tennessee Normal, 1913-19; Head of Agricultural Department Union University, 1919-

GEORGE EARLY SHANKLE, A. M.

Chair of English

Graduate of Dickson College; Hall-Moody Institute; A. B. Union University, 1917; A. M. University, 1918; M. O. Union University, 1919; Graduate student University of Tennessee; Tulane University; A. M. Peabody, 1922; Residence work finished in George Peabody College for Ph. D. degree; five years Principal of Public Schools; three years Professor in Hall-Moody Institute; Chair' of English Union University, 1919-.

J. N. MALLORY, A. M., Ph: D.

Professor of Mathematics

Graduate North Texas State Normal; A. B. Oklahoma University; A. M. Baylor University; Fifteen years Principal of Public Schools in Texas; Chair Science, College of Marshall, 1917-19; Chair Mathematics, Union University, 1919-21; Ph. D., Peabody College, 1922.

J. R. MANTEY, Th. M., Th. D.

Chair of Greek

A. B. William Jewell; Th. M., Southwestern Baptist Theological Seminary; Th. D., Southern Baptist Theological Seminary; Professor in Southwestern Theological Seminary two years; Author of articles in The Expositor (London); Joint author of "A Manual of the Greek New Testament"; member of The Society of Biblical Literature and Exegesis; President of The American Research Society; Chair of Greek in Union University 1922-

L. DeWITT RUTLEDGE, A. M.

Chair of History and Economics

A. B., in Education, Valparaiso, 1914; A. M., Union University, 1917; (Graduate student for Ph. D. degree George Peabody), A. M. Peabody 1923; Principal West Point Collegiate Institute, 1899-1900; Principal Waterloo High School, 1901-05; Principal Doyle Institute, 1907-10; Principal Bridgeport Academy, 1911-14; Chair of Latin Hall-Moody Institute, 1914-16; Chair of History, Union University, 1916-

JAMES LUTHER McALILEY, A. M.

Chair of Latin
Bursar

A. B. Union University, 1915; seven years Principal of Public Schools; Principal of Union Academy, 1915-16; Graduate student Baylor University, 1919; A. M. Union University, 1920; Graduate student Peabody College, 1920; Head of Latin, Union University, 1916-

WILLIAM WALLACE DUNN, A. M.

Chair of Physics

Graduate of Hall-Moody Institute, 1906; Student Tennessee University, 1906-7; Chair of Science and Mathematics Hall-Moody Institute, 1907-10; Superintendent of Halls City Schools, 1910-13; Student Vanderbilt-Peabody, 1913-16; Finished A. B. Course in Vanderbilt; Received A. M. degree from George Peabody College in 1916; Superintendent of Trenton City Schools, 1916-17; Professor of Physics Union University, 1918-

I. N. PENICK, Th. M., D. D.

Chair of Theology and Evangelism

A. B. Union University, 1896; Th. M., Southwestern Baptist Theological Seminary, 1921; twenty-two years pastor of First Baptist Church, Martin, Tennessee; sixteen years editor of Baptist Builder; Author of books and tracts; Summer School instructor in Southwestern Baptist Theological Seminary summer terms 1919, 1920 1921, 1922.

MISS MYRTLE SAVIDGE

A. B. University of Minnesota; Graduate student University of Chicago, Ill.; Graduate of the Emerson School of Oratory; Eleven years experience in Teaching.

MRS. ARTHUR WARREN PRINCE, B. M., M. M.

Director of Music

Graduate and Post-Graduate of Piano under Jno. B. Kindig of Germany, 1899-1900; Chicago Artists, 1902; Pipe Organ under D. S. DeLisle of St. Louis University, 1905-08; Private studio work, 1905-08; Organist of First Baptist Church since 1909; Student with Herio Levy of American Conservatory, 1908-09; Director of Union Conservatory, 1910-

JAMES WORK,

Voice

MISS CHARLOTTE H. WATSON

Home Economics

Graduate University of Wisconsin; Chair Home Economics, Meridian Woman's College, Mississippi, and schools in Michigan.

MISS GRACE POWERS, A. B.
(Union University)
(A Smith-Hughes Teacher)
First Assistant in Home Economics

MISS CLARA GILBERT
(Union University)
Second Assistant in Home Economics

MISS VIVIAN WHITEHEAD, A. M.
A. B. Union University, 1916; A. M. Union University, 1921.
Spanish

MISS VERA ROUTON
Assistant in Spanish

J. W. STOVALL, A. B.
Curator of the Museum, and Assistant in Biology

HARRY CARTER
Secretary Alumni Association,
President Students' Booster Club

RAYMOND GUYON
Concert Violinist, Conductor, Theorist
Director of Band and Orchestra

MRS. GWENDOLYN STEPHENSON GUYON
Clarinetist, Cornetist, Saxophonist, Conductor, Composer

MRS. EMMA WATERS SUMMAR
Cook County Normal
Librarian

MISS GLADYS McMINN
MISS LUCIE MAI SILER
Assistant Librarians

MISS LOUISE BENGE
Registrar

MISS VERA ROUTON
Bookkeeper

J. L. McALILEY
Bursar

MISS VIVIAN WHITELAW
Secretary to the President

LABORATORY ASSISTANTS
HAL CARTER, Chemistry
GEO. MALONE, Chemistry
PRINT HUDSON, A. B.

MARTIN DAVIS, B. S.
Assistant in Vocational Agriculture

MRS. MATTIE MAER
Dining Hall Superintendent and Matron Lovelace Hall.

MRS. W. W. DUNN
Matron Adams Hall.

B. O. WOLFE
Superintendent of Buildings and Grounds
(For faculties of Training School and Business College see pages 91, 93)

General Information

THE OPENING

The formal opening of the University will take place at 10:00 a. m., Tuesday, September 18. It is desired that applicants meet the faculty in offices Monday and Tuesday, September 17th and 18th, to take their entrance examinations or present their certificates from accredited schools and secure their registration. It is possible for all students to have registered, received their tickets of studies, settled their fees, located themselves in their boarding places, and to be ready for class-room work on the 18th immediately after the formal opening. The administration insists on this being done.

All inquiries for information about entrance, course of study, expenses, scholarships, etc., should be made to the President.

Remittances for current expenses should be made to J. L. McAliley, Bursar of the University.

THE CITY OF JACKSON

Union University is located in Jackson, Tennessee, almost midway betweeen Mobile and St. Louis on the Mobile and Ohio Railroad; between Chicago and New Orleans, on the Illinois Central Railroad; between Memphis and Nashville, and Paducah and Memphis on the Nashville, Chattanooga and St. Louis Railroad. Jackson is connected with Dyersburg by the Birmingham and Northwestern Railway, with Birmingham and Jacksonville by another Illinois Central line, and also connected with the Gulf by the Gulf, Mobile & Northern. See map on front page.

Counting arrivals and departures, Jackson now has thirty daily trains. Nearly all these trains arrive and leave between 5:30 a. m. and 8 p. m. This is wonderful with a place having so many roads. Ministerial students will especially notice the advantages of transportation afforded them to reach churches on or near nine lines of railroad. About one hundred churches are thus served by pastors each year.

Jackson is a progressive city of twenty-five thousand inhabitants, distinguished for hospitality, beautiful residences and parks. There is an extensive system of pikes in all directions, which together with the three National Highways intersecting here, makes the University very accessible by auto and carriage service.

Though industries abound and prosper, it is peculiarly a city of homes and flowers, a place of culture and refinement, alike attractive to the resident, the visitor, and the student. Many families have moved here primarily for superior educational advantages.

HEALTHFULNESS

That Jackson is healthful is attested by the low death rate—a condition due in no small degree to the complete system of sanitation and the purity of the water supply. Coming from thirty-six artesian wells, this water supply seems inexhaustible, and is conveyed to all parts of the corporation by efficient municipal control.

A wonderful artesian well of fine sulphur and electro-chalybeate water is one of the attractions of Jackson.

The elevation of the spacious campus, covered with grass and shaded with large oaks, the thick walls of the buildings, and long, wide halls and large windows, make Union University a splendid site for a summer school, which is maintained each year with rapidly growing popularity.

THE STUDENT COUNCIL

The Student Council assists the faculty in discipline and has complete responsibility of enforcing the "Honor System." It is composed of five faculty members, five young men and five young women elected by the student body.

A similar body is elected in each of the halls to take care of the discipline in each hall.

These committees have brought about a very fine spirit and high standard of conduct among the students.

GOVERNMENT

Union has a co-operative form of student government. The students co-operate with the faculty through the Student Council described above.

It is assumed that all who attend the University know right from wrong conduct, and that they are disposed to do the right. This is not a reform school, and parents must not expect us to do for their children, in matters of discipline, what they themselves have failed to do, and young men and women must not expect to shift from their own shoulders the responsibility of right living. Neither must they expect the University to tolerate unmanly or unwomanly conduct. Self-control ought to be the aim of every student and is the ideal which the University sets before them.

The University cannot accept full responsibility for the home conduct and social life of those students who attend the University from local homes. Parents and the students themselves must be responsible for such conduct when off the campus.

The University offers boarding accommodations for one hundred twenty-five young women and one hundred twenty-five young men on the campus.

The school can and does accept a measure of responsibility to the parents for those students committed to our care who board in the college buildings; but manifestly, the school cannot accept full responsibility for the outside social conduct of those who board in private homes. The school will keep a list of approved private boarding places, and when parents request it, will recommend them to students; but aside from the advantage in economy, there are many reasons why we recommend that all students who can secure rooms, should board in the University buildings.

Parents ought to require that their children board on the campus, and students under twenty-one years of age will not be allowed to board in private homes without written consent of parents. Students must not change boarding places without the consent of the president, and such consent will be given only when satisfactory reason is shown. Arrangements may be made, when satisfactory reason can be given, for their rooming in private homes and taking meals at the college dining hall, or for taking rooms in the college halls and meals in private homes, but boys and girls are not allowed to room or eat at the same private place.

Girls will not be permitted to board or room in private homes except as follows, with near relatives, or with faculty members. The faculty may make exceptions in special cases, but rarely.

Students of college age and grade may be safely entrusted with more liberties than the average high-school student. Our government is designed mostly for college or mature students, therefore young and immature academy students (boys) do not fit well into our form of discipline, consequently we cannot accept them for boarders in Adams Hall. *Students needing constant watching should be sent elsewhere.*

While it is manifestly impossible for the faculty to know all the breaches of right conduct, or to prevent them, yet an earnest endeavor will be made to enforce the following:

FUNDAMENTAL REGULATIONS

First. Absentees from classes will be expected to make up each recitation with a coach or an assistant in that department. This applies also to students who enter a few days late in any term. Those who enter later in the term may not expect full credit for a term's work in any subject. In some instances where the teachers deem it proper, a few hours' credit may be given in such cases. *Ten unexcused absences or tardies will automatically suspend one from school.*

Second. Students are not permitted to give entertainments during the college session, either on the campus or in the name of the school or any department or any organization of it in the city without consent of the President or faculty committee.

Third. Students whose college standing is unsatisfactory are forbidden to appear in any University function of a public nature. This applies to athletics as well as to literary celebrations and to oratorical contests.

Fourth. Except by special faculty consent, students must attempt to take not more than seventeen hours a term. Only in very exceptional cases will this consent be granted.

Fifth. Keeping concealed weapons, swearing, playing cards or dice, or drinking spirituous liquors, are absolutely forbidden. Visiting pool rooms is forbidden under penalty of expulsion.

Sixth. Hazing will receive severest penalty.

Seventh. Students are forbidden to seek aid in examination, other than that given by the instructor in charge, upon penalty of expulsion. The Honor System under the control of the Student Council is in vogue.

Eighth. No clubs, fraternities or societies may be formed unless the faculty, on application, approve the design of such organization, the rules by which it proposes to be governed, and the hours of the meeting. The faculty reserves the right to limit or to disband any such organizations.

Ninth. The following classes of students shall be eligible to membership in any fraternity or sorority:

(a) All college students, excepting freshmen who are conditioned in more than one subject required for entrance, and those who have not passed all their work for the term preceding nomination.

(b) Any special student, meeting college entrance requirements, who is carrying at least twelve hours strictly college work, and who has passed all his work of the term preceding nomination.

NOTE: Fraternities and sororities must have faculty consent to initiate any student, and thirty days must be given the faculty for investigation before this consent will be given.

Tenth. No student will be allowed to deliver the same oration in more than one contest.

Eleventh. Students must be quiet and orderly in their boarding houses, and thoughtful of the rights of others. Going to town during study hours or at nights is disorderly and is therefore forbidden. Occasions may arise which justify a seeming violation of this rule. Young men are put on their honor, but subject themselves to being called to account for being out of room or being seen in town enough to arouse suspicion in the minds of friends. The wholesome restraint of wise, strong, affectionate parents, in family life, constitute safe regulations.

Twelfth. While the faculty cannot assume the responsibility of boarding students not on the campus, it reserves the right to make such regulations at any time as may seem advisable, and the violations of the regulations on the part of a student will deprive him of the privileges of the school.

Thirteenth.—Beginning with this year the faculty will deal with all of the student organizations in the matter of discipline as with individuals, viz: assess demerits which shall carry a stated punishment. These shall be cumulative through the year.

DISCIPLINE IN THE HALLS

The rooms and furniture of both halls are to be gone over thoroughly and be put into first-class condition, and rigid rules will be enforceed to keep them in this condition. The deposit required of every one is to guarantee that all breakage and damage will be made good. The student, together with the superintendent of the hall, will make a careful inventory of everything in the room and its condition, both on entering and on leaving it. Each student will be held responsible for his own room, and all collectively will be held for all property and parts of the building. The deposit will be returned at the close of the year less any claim for damage.

All students on entering any of the halls, voluntarily and tacitly agree to obey all rules of conduct and deportment that govern the halls.

Lovelace Hall has a modified form of student government under the supervision of Mrs. Maer and Dr. Mallory.

Strict discipline and good order will be maintained. Those who are unwilling to co-operate in maintaining good order would better not enter. It will save them trouble and embarrassment later.

Adams Hall has student government under the supervision of Prof. Dunn and wife, who live in the hall, and this form of government is growing in popularity and efficiency.

RESERVING ROOMS

Anyone who wishes to reserve a room in either of the halls for the coming school year may do so by seeing the President in person or by writing to him, designating the room and making a deposit of $5.00, which will be placed on the room ticket. This ticket will be retained by the Bursar, and the student may settle the balance at the opening of the school and receive the ticket.

NOTE.—Room reservation is not refunded. The reason is obvious, and patrons will please not embarrass us by asking for exceptions.

NOTE

Boys and Girls taking their meals in private homes must eat at separate boarding places.

This is a new rule, made necessary by the conduct of students in the past. Students must not ask for the privilege of violating this rule. The best interests of the school and student body demand that we enforce this rule rigidly.

RELIGIOUS LIFE

This institution is not a reformatory nor a theological school, neither is it a gymnasium. On another page we have mentioned the emphasis placed upon the training of the body. It is not necessary to mention the emphasis placed upon the training of the mind. But we would emphasize the fact that we are anxious not to neglect the training of the spirit, the cultivation and development of the moral and religious nature, because a finely trained mind in a well-developed body all goes for naught if the soul is lost. This school is not a church, nor a prayer-meeting; yet we are careful that a healthful religious atmosphere shall so far as possible pervade the entire institution. In chapel exercises, in class rooms, in every relation where the occasion arises, something is said or done to remind the student that after all, the religious life is best, that the Bible is true, and that that life only is worth living which is ordered according to its precepts.

There are religious organizations among the students:

First: The J. R. G. Society, exclusively for young ministers, which has its session every Friday afternoon for discussion of religious topics. This Society has made a wonderful contribution to the religious development of the South.

Second. The Volunteer Band, which meets weekly for the study of missions and other religious topics.

A healthy Christian atmosphere pervades the entire institution and during the year many students decide for Christ, and others become settled in their convictions as to their duty in religious work.

The students conduct a weekly college prayer-meeting in the chapel or halls.

A revival is conducted each year at some time during the session. In the revival conducted the past session by Dr. J. E. Skinner resulted most happily. Many were saved, while a still larger number re-dedicated their lives to the Lord for special religious services.

Buildings and Equipment

The following statement as to the value of the University property is taken from the auditor's statement:

Endowment $140,000
Buildings and land 470,000
Equipment 34,193

Total	$645,873

The Executive Board of the Tennessee Baptist Convention appropriates $18,000 each year to the college for current expenses, and as much more for equipment and indebtedness, which is equivalent to the income from an endowment of $700,000.

Campus

The campus of the University, containing fifteen acres, is located in the east part of the city within three blocks of the business district. On it are situated the eight buildings of the University. Mr. C. C. Combs, landscape artist of St. Louis, was recently employed to go over the campus and make plans and specifications for improving it, converting it into a beautiful park. To carry out a part of his suggestions, many hundred dollars worth of shrubs were planted according to blue prints, by the students on a holiday. These improvements, together with many others, have already made the campus one of the beauty spots of Jackson.

Buildings

Before any student will be allowed to move into any room in either of the halls, he will be required to see the Bursar, choose his room, make satisfactory settlement, and receive his room ticket, which he will show to the proper person at the hall. For this ticket he will pay the price of the room rent for the term. The charge is so small that there will be no refund for time out.

Adams Hall

On August 13, 1918, the front part of Adams Hall was destroyed by fire, but has been rebuilt, and made better and more modern than before. The parlors, halls and bed rooms are beautiful. The rooms are new, fresh, have commodious closets, have been newly furnished and are very inviting. Twelve of the rooms are connected with private baths, and shower baths are located on each floor convenient to the other rooms.

The east wing has been made fresh and inviting.

Few, if any schools in the State, can offer better rooming accommodations for young men than Union now offers. Students will furnish their own bed linen, pillows, covering, and toilet articles.

Everett Lovelace Hall

The dormitory for young women is a splendid three-story building completed in 1897. In this hall rooms are provided at a minimum cost for about sixty young women. The furniture of the rooms consist of chairs, a table, washstand, dresser, bed and mattress, bowl and pitcher. Each room has a very large closet. Young women should bring with them blankets, quilts, sheets, pillow cases, towels, and napkins. Only two students occupy a room.

On each floor are bathrooms with hot and cold water, closets and lavatories. The building is heated with hot water, and lighted by electricity. It is under the strict, but kind management of Mrs. Maer.

Many important changes and improvements are to be made in this hall this year. The dining hall and kitchen will be removed and converted into bed rooms, the parlors will be changed to the opposite side of the building, the rooms re-papered and many other improvements will be made.

Dining Hall

The building known as Dorcas Hall, formerly the Conservatory, will be remodeled into a dining hall, to accommodate 250.

Barton Hall

The new administration building is located on the site of the old one. It is modern in every appointment and classic in design. It contains the library and reading room, recitation rooms, society and fraternity rooms, and administration office. Immediately behind the main building and connected with it is the chapel hall with a seating capacity of five hundred. The equipment throughout is complete and modern. There are few better equipped college buildings anywhere in the South.

Power House

This is a building of light brick, erected in 1905, and situated at a safe and convenient distance from Adams Hall, Barton Hall, and Powell Chapel. It contains a battery of two boilers and a complete electric light plant.

Library and Reading Room

In the administration building the Library and Reading Room is furnished splendid quarters. There are about ten thousand volumes well selected and catalogued, including the T. T. Eaton bequest, which givese us a good working library, to which additions are made each year. The reading room contains the leading magazines, religious periodicals and daily papers. The order kept here is almost perfect, no better in any city library.

In addition to this, the Jackson Free Public Library of 25,000 volumes is within three blocks of the University, on College Street; and pupils have free access to it.

These libraries give our students splendid library facilities.

Athletic Field

A new field for athletics has been acquired and put in good condition on the square adjoining the campus on the east.

Gymnasium

The new gymnasium is nearing completion. It is a splendid building, 77x92 feet, and contains two courts 77x40 feet, one for boys, one for girls, with showers and lockers for both.

Joseph A. Crook Hall

The new girls' home on the south campus has been christened the Joseph A. Crook Hall, in memory of the late Dr. J. A. Crook, who was a member of the Board of Trustees for forty years, was secretary most of that time, and was one of the most loyal supporters the school ever had. This is nearing completion and will accommodate sixty girls and house the Home Economics Department. The bed rooms will be beautiful and well-lighted; all except two rooms will have two windows, and six will have four. Provisions will be made for about half of the girls to do their own cooking or clubbing.

Museum

Most of the collections that had been made were destroyed when the main building burned in 1912. We are now trying to start a museum worthy of the institution. The first gift of any consequence was made some years ago by Mr. J. D. Barnett, Forrest City, Ark., A. B. of the class of 1886. This is a very valuable collection of geological, historical, and biological relics and specimens, and makes a fine nucleus around which we hope to build a splendid museum.

To these have been added valuable contributions by other alumni; one by Rev. J. Frank Ray, D. D., class of 1902, now in Shimonoseki, Japan. This collection contains many things of interest from that quaint and interesting country.

Another is a valuable collection from the battle front, brought back by Captain Julius Johnson, class of 1911.

The other by Sergeant Harry Carter of the Rainbow Division, and Alvin Todd of the Navy, some interesting things from Germany, and the Philippine Islands.

For the past year Mr. J. W. Stovall has been busy collecting and classifying material, and has made a remarkable showing. He received two valuable shipments from the Smithsonian Institute, and many things from friends in various lands. The most valuable addition was an indefinite loan of the great private collection of Indian and Mound Builder relics of Judge Homer Tatum of Alamo. There are about five thousand specimens, most of them catalogued.

We hope that all the old students and friends of the institution everywhere will follow the example set by these loyal alumni and friends and make contributions. Since our students and friends are scattered all over the world, if each one would send a few things from his own locality, we would soon have a splendid museum.

If the friends do not feel like making an absolute donation, we will be glad to pay expenses on geological specimens, plants, animals, and relics of various kinds. If any friend possesses or knows of things of special value that will require some initial cost, we hope they will correspond with us about it. We shall be glad for friends to make us loans of things of special interest.

The City Y. M. C. A.

The City Y. M. C. A., a hundred thousand dollar building, is located three squares from the University campus. It contains a splendid gymnasium and swimming pool, which are at the disposal of the students for a nominal sum.

MEDALS

A gold medal, established by Festus Rhodes for the best orator in the Calliopean Society.

The Calliopean Society gives each year a gold medal for the most general improvement in proficiency in debate, also a "best debater's" medal.

The Joseph H. Eaton Medal for Oratory, established by Dr. T. T. Eaton and continued by his sister, Mrs. Joe E. Peck, Murfreesboro, Tenn., in honor of their father, Union's first president.

A gold medal given by W. G. Foster for best orator in Apollonian Society. Also best debater's and loyalty medals, given by Apollonian Society.

The J. W. Porter award of an International Dictionary or a Liddell and Scott's Unabridged Greek Dictionary for the best essay on some assigned topic, limited to the members of the J. R. Graves Society of Religious Inquiry.

The Fannie Forrester Medal, established by G. M. Savage, is given to the pupil who contemplates most satisfactorily the postgraduate course in music according to the decision of the director of the Conservatory.

The Charles H. Strickland Medal, established by Mrs. C. H. Strickland for the best orator in the Senior Class. This is an endowed medal, and therefore permanent.

The Elizabeth Tigrett Medal founded by I. B. Tigrett in honor of his mother. It is awarded to the Senior who has, in the opinion of the faculty, made the best record during the year in college. Scholarship and usefulness in student activitiees are the tests emphasized. The student must be a member of some literary society. This medal carries with it the highest honors of the Senior class.

A gold medal is given by M. M. Summar to that member of the Academy Class winning highest honors based on the following:

1st. Scholarship as judged by grades made during year, consideration being given amount of work carried.

2nd. Interest manifested in the various school activities.

3rd. Loyalty and school spirit.

Loyalty Medal founded by Mrs. M. M. Summar for the Palladian Society.

The Karrie Karnes Barry Medal for the best essay in the Palladian Society.

The A. W. Prince Medal given for the best article for the year in the Cardinal and Cream.

Rev. J. G. Hughes, Quannah, Texas, class of 1917, has established a medal which will be given the Senior delivering the best oration at the August commencement.

Student Organization.

Student Organizations

The University is not responsible for any financial obligation
incurred by a student organization, student, member
of faculty, or employee unless authorized
by the President in writing.

STUDENT ACTIVITY ASSOCIATION

The Student Activity Association controls the finances in a large measure of a number of subordinate organizations. This body has control of the ways and means of financing these organizations, and is under the management of the students themselves. It handles all the books and stationery of the school, the profits to be used as the student body may direct in financing their several activities. This organization arranges for collective buying, handles the laundry and has control of practically all of the financially profitable enterprises in which the students may collectively engage. The funds of the organization are used as the students may direct: to help needy students, to finance the Athletic Association, to assist in financing the Cardinal and Cream, the Annual, and such other enterprises as the students themselves may vote to foster.

ATHLETIC ASSOCIATION

This association promotes and fosters teams and games in football, basketball, baseball, and tennis. It stands for and insists upon clean and wholesome athletics and has maintained very high standards. Through its high standards and influence, young men are toned up in their moral character and ideals, and even in their religious views.

ATHLETICS

Union University believes in training the body as well as the mind and soul. Perhaps nothing encourages an interest in physical exercise more than college athletics. While it usually happens that those who are on the teams are already devloped, and therefore do not need the inter-collegiate contests for their own physical growth, yet it is true that most of them were originally aroused to an interest in the development of their bodies either by participating in games, or by watching the games of others. Thus it is that physical contests of all kinds call attention to the need of caring for and training the body, and arouse interest in such training. Inter-collegiate contests and the publicity given them constantly remind teachers, parents and young people themselves that physical training is one of the necessary preparations for a complete life; and without these constant reminders, such training would be seriously neglected. But if it were not entirely neglected, without these contests the training would lose much of its interest and zest, which are so vitally essential to its greatest success. For these and other reasons athletics, while at first misunderstood, often misdirected and frequently corrupted, was subjected to very severe criticism and met much opposition. But its true merits have so won out, so many of the objectionable features have been eliminated, its character and object have become so much better understood, its redeeming qualities so much more appreciated, that today athletics is almost universally approved, and only a comparatively few objectors remain.

The world has recently had a wonderful demonstration of the influence of athletics upon national character. For example, Germany had no athletics—had no games. Her boys and people were not taught in youthful contests to "give and take." They were not taught the meaning of the word "fair play" in a struggle with a contestant. To understand the results, contrast their national character as demonstrated in their inconsiderate and cruel conduct of the war with the daring, courageous, yet chivalrous spirit of America, as illustrated by her school boy army which knew how to fight, and yet knew how to consider the common rights of humanity, even of an enemy—in other words, knew how to "play fair." One was the result of physical training without athletics, and the other character and physical training with and through athletics.

In order that our college teams may be a credit to the institution, and that it will be a compliment to a young man to be a member of the team, the faculty has adopted the following rules which will be strictly adhered to:

1. None but *bona fide* students of this institution shall be allowed to participate in inter-collegiate or inter-scholastic contests.

By "bona fide" student is meant:

(a) Any student who is carrying a regular course of study of not fewer than twelve hours a week in this institution, and who was enrolled at or near the first of the term in which he plays.

(b) Any student who has failed or been conditioned on no more than one-third of his work.

(c) Any student who during the session does not absent himself from classes unless excused by the President.

2. No team will be allowed to be absent from the University for more than four recitation days during a season.

3. A member of the faculty shall accompany all teams when away from the University.

4. Before closing dates for games it shall be the business of the Manager of each team to submit a list of the games with dates to the Coach and President for approval.

5. The Managers will be held responsible for the return of all equipment charged to them, who in turn shall so hold each student to whom they issue equipment.

6. *All funds shall pass through the books in the College office and all checks be signed by the President, and the President shall approve all contracts or orders involving money. This is imperative.*

All athletics is now under the general control of a council of three faculty members, two alumni and four students elected by the student body.

LITERARY SOCIETIES

The literary societies play a prominent part in the life of the student body. There are three for boys, the Apollonian, Calliopean, and the G. M. Savage Societies. The last named organized two years ago, the other two have been in existence for nearly three-quarters of a century. There are two for girls, the Palladian Literary Society, organized fifty years ago, and the Eonian, organized two years ago and named for Miss Ena Williams. These societies are flourishing, wide-awake, have handsomely furnished rooms and meet weekly.

CARDINAL AND CREAM

This is a weekly college paper edited and published by the students and is a bright, breezy, readable paper. Sample copies will be sent upon request.

"LEST WE FORGET"

This is a magnificent book, well bound, and issued every other year by the students. It contains a vast array of pictures, and breezy, catchy bits of literary work. It is a volume always greatly prized by the students, and one that grows in value with the passinig years.

FRATERNITIES AND SORORITIES

Union has two fraternities—Alpha Tau Omega, and Sigma Alpha Epsilon—and one sorority—Sigma Sigma Sigma. They have their own special activities and functions, and add variety and charm to the college life.

THE DEBATERS' LEAGUE

This is a new organization intended to promote public speaking in the form of debates only. It arranges and prepares for inter-collegiate contests. A simultaneous debate is held each year with Carson and Newman College. The past year our teams met Wake Forest College and Louisiana College.

THE NESTOR CLUB

This is a special literary club of upper-classmen consisting of thirteen members, one of whom is a member of the faculty, and is organized to promote special scholastic interest and attainments. When a vacancy is caused by the graduation of some member, a new member is elected his successor from the upper-classmen.

HYPATIA CLUB.

This is a literary and social club of upper class girls, limited to eighteen in number, and is intended to train the girls for success in such clubs after they leave school.

OTHER CLUBS

"The Aggies," composed of agricultural students.

"The Chem Club," composed of chemical fans.

"The Home Ec," composed of girls in the Home Economics Department.

"The Doctors," composed of pre-medical students. All these clubs meet with a program every two weeks and discuss topics of peculiar interest to those of the group. They create and maintain a vital interest in each department represented.
Expenses

Expenses

The school year is divided into three terms both for the re-adjustment of classes and for the payment of fees.

The amounts designated below are due and payable at the beginning of their respective terms. Tuition is NOT charged for by the month, but by the year, the amount for the year being divided according to the terms for convenience.

ALL fees MUST be settled with the Bursar before a student will be enrolled in any class. The student who cannot pay cash must see the Bursar and make satisfactory arrangements before entering classes, just as those paying cash.

If a student cannot pay any or all of his fees when they are due, he should come prepared to make a bankable note, or other satisfactory arrangement.

A small laboratory fee is charged each student who works in the laboratory, to cover the cost of re-agents consumed. This in the past has averaged $5 a term for Chemistry and $3 a term each for other sciences.

Ministers of all denominations pay for their children one-half the regular tuition fees in the college and academy.

No boarding students will be allowed to carry fewer than fourteen hours work, except on advice of physician.

TABLE OF EXPENSES

	First Term	Second Term	Third Term
Literary Tuition—			
Regular rate after ten days......................	$38.00	$26.00	$26.00
Cash one term in advance........................	34.00	25.00	25.00
Cash in advance for first two terms............			54.00
Cash in advance for last two terms.............			46.00
Cash in advance for whole year (3 terms).....			77.00
Fees in Home Economics Department—			
Cooking	$ 8.50	$ 7.50	$ 7.50
Sewing	6.00	5.00	5.00
Home Decoration (if taken alone)...............	3.00	2.00	2.00
Full Economics Course	14.00	12.00	12.00
Cooking one year in advance			$20.00
Sewing one year in advance			14.00
Full course one year in advance			32.00

N o t e:—Students taking Home Economics but no Literary work will pay in addition to the above fees, the regular matriculation fees, and ten dollars a term tuition.

Table Board—			
Regular rate after ten days......................	$72.00	$57.00	$57.00
Cash one term in advance........................	70.00	55.00	55.00
Cash in advance first two terms................			$120.00

Cash in advance last two terms...............			155.00
Cash in advance whole year (3 terms)........			170.00
Matriculation fees ....$ 6.00		$ 6.00	$ 6.00
Matriculation fees one year in advance.......			15.00
Student activity fees 4.00		4.00	4.00
Student activity fees one year in advance......			10.00

If any student spends more than the above amounts parents should investigate and write the President in regard to it.

Girls' Club

Expenses in the Girls' Club are much less. Girls can easily make their expenses less than the above by more than $100. Write for information.

Occupants of the dormitories who have keys to their doors, are not permitted to exchange keys with one another when they change rooms. All keys must be bruoght to the office and exchanged. Absolutely no refund will be allowed for a key bearing a number different from that issued. Room Rents (Each person, one term in advance)—

	First Term	Second Term	Third Term
Adams Hall, East Wing $12.00		$10.00	$10.00

Rooms without bath, $10 to $16 a term.
Rooms with bath, $12 to $18 a term.

Girls' Halls—

For one-window room.......................$12.00		$10.00	$10.00
For two-window room........................ 14.00		12.00	12.00
For three-window room...................... 17.00		14.00	14.00
For four-window room....................... 19.00		16.00	16.00

Cash two terms in advance 6% discount on the second term.

Cash three terms in advance 8% discount on the second and third terms.

Room Reservation.—We have only a limited number of rooms and for the past three years they have been engaged before the opening of school. This has necessitated our requiring a reservation fee of $5· which is not refunded, but transferred to room rent when student enters.

Books and stationery estimated—varies from $15 to $30 a year. Laundry, from $15 to $30 a year.

CONDENSED TABLE OF EXPENSES

	Cash 1 Year in Advance.	Cash at 1st of Each Term.	At close of Each Term
Tuition ....$ 77.00		$ 84.00	$ 90.00
Board 170.00		180.00	186.00
Matriculation 15.00		18.00	18.00
Room Rent (minimum) 28.00		32.00	32.00
Students' Fees 10.00		12.00	12.00
Total $300.00		$326.00	$338.00

Remark.—It will be observed that the cash discount is sufficient to enable a student to save money by borrowing money for his entire expenses at 8%. Or in other words, the school pays the interest for the student who borrows money and pays cash.

The discount really amounts to approximately 14%, since more than one-third of the whole amount is due in advance anyway, one-third in three months, and the balance in six months. It is therefore highly profitable for all to pay in advance.

Remark II.—Where students pay two or more terms in advance, and find it necessary to leave school, proportionate refunds are made. For example, if student leaves at close of first term, he will be charged for the first term at the rate quoted for "one term in advance" and be refunded the balance. Students leaving at close of second term will be charged at the rate quoted for "two terms in advance," and be refunded the balance. Students leaving before the closing of a term will be settled with according to the above statements (modified by the refund rules governing fraction of terms).

Remark III.—*Heat and Lights.* Students rooming in the halls, but taking meals off the campus will pay three dollars a month additional for water, heat and lights. In the spring and summer terms the rate is $1.50. These rates also apply to the girls doing their own cooking. These fees are charged because the cost of heat, water, and lights is charged in the account for board, and not in the account for room rent.

Fee for Students' Activities $10 a year, or $4 a term. This is turned over to the Students' Council to finance their activities, and among other things includes a year's subscription to the Cardinal and Cream, Lyceum ticket, and admittance to all games.

TUITION IN FINE ARTS

	First Term	Second Term	Third Term
Piano (Advanced, under director)	$30.00	$25.00	$25.00
Piano (Intermediate, under director)	26.00	22.00	22.00
Piano (Primary)	22.00	19.00	19.00
*Voice	30.00	25.00	25.00
Pipe Organ—Same as in Piano.			
Sight Singing	8.00	6.00	6.00
Gospel Music Course	4.00	3.00	3.00
Composition and Advanced Theory—			
(Private lessons)	$12.00	$ 9.00	$ 9.00
Harmony (In class)	8.00	8.00	8.00
Musical History	8.00	8.00	8.00
Expression (Private lessons)	21.00	15.00	15.00
Piano Rent, one hour a day, each	6.00	4.00	4.00
Additional hour a day	4.00	3.00	3.00

TERMS

Violin, per year $70.00
Other string instruments.. 60.00
Clarinet, per year.. 70.00
Other wood-wind instruments... 60.00
Cornet or trumpet... 70.00
Percussion instruments, including instruction in double-drumming and
Other brass instruments... 60.00
Percussion instruments, including instruction in double-drumming and
    bell playing 70.00
Saxophone 70.00

GRADUATION FEES

College Department $10.00
Music Department 10.00
Expression Department 5.00
Academy Department 5.00
Home Economics 5.00

NOTICE

All students in all departments must get a matriculation card from the President's office and pay matriculation fees at the Bursar's desk. The teachers must insist upon each pupil presenting a matriculation card stamped by the Bursar.

*A discount in Voice of 10% will be made for cash one year in advance, and an additional discount of 10% will be made for students taking full literary work.

Change of Classes

It is detrimental to the school and usually to the individual student to change classes after once entered, and so to compensate the loss to the school and to. reduce to the minimum these changes, in keeping with the policy of the best institutions, we will hereafter make the following charges for each change:

First week, 25c; second week, 50c; after second week, $1.00. A change means: to drop a class, to tak up a new one, or to exchange classes.

No change can be made without the written consent of the Professor or Professors concerned, the President, or in his absence, the Dean, and the permit must bear the Bursar's stamp. Any infraction of this rule subjects the student to a fine of $2, and such additional punishment as the case may demand.

Refunds

Room rents, matriculation fees, and room reservation fees are never refunded. Board is refunded for absence of even weeks, no fractions of a week considered.

Tuition is refunded in the Literary Department, provided that no refund will be considered for less than one month's absence in any term, and full month's tuition will be charged for any fraction of a month that the student may be in attendance.

The claim for refund will be considered only from the date Bursar is notified in writing of absence. Where possible the Bursar should be notified in advance. No claim may be made for time preceding such notification. Reasons for these rules are obvious.

The Business School, in keeping with all other first-class business colleges, in consideration of the reduced price, makes no refund on scholarships. Those not willing to risk the price of a

scholarship should accept and pay the monthly rate.   For rates
and terms write Mr. C. A. Derryberry.

It will be observed that all of the above rules and regulations
put the responsibility upon the pupil.   He saves money by seeing
the President and Bursar immediately.   Delays and negligence
are costly.   Students should learn to be prompt.

Deposit Fees

Every student entering one of the boarding halls must deposit
a breakage fee of $5.00, and a key deposit of $1.00.   Students
in Chemistry will deposit a breakage fee of $5.00.

These deposit fees will be returned to the student upon leaving
school or at the close of the year, or upon return of articles, less
any loss or damage charges.

Tutors

Students required to meet a tutor in any department will pay
fifty cents for each lesson.

Remarks on Ministerial Education

The ministerial board will consider all contributions placed in
its hands as a *loan fund,* to be lent, not given, to those who need
help.   The personal note of the student will be taken, to begin
bearing three per cent interest two years after the student leaves
school.   No security will be required except for three brethren,
pastors or deacons, will sign an attached statement that they have
implicit faith in the student's sincerity, piety, and honest regard
for moral obligations.

This is done for two reasons: First, to protect the ministerial
students from unjust criticism and at the same time have regard
for and develop their sense of self-respect.   Second, to enable the
University to develop in the course of years a large loan fund
that will assist a much larger body of struggling young preachers.   The young preachers themselves welcome this change.   The
worthy ones will be only too glad to pay back the debt to help
someone else, and the one who will object to doing so is unwor-
thy of the sacrifice of the churches in supporting him.

LOAN FUNDS

Walter Gray Fund

In August, 1918, Mrs. Sallie Patrick of Collierville, Tennessee,
gave the University a sum of money to be used as a fund to be
loaned worthy students in memory of her deceased son, Walter
Gray.   The trustees accepted this and named it the Walter Gray

Fund. In the first year it enabled nine of the best students in school to continue through the year. All of these otherwise would have been compelled to drop out of school. Some of them have since graduated and are holding good positions. Others are still in school. Mrs. Patrick was so well pleased with the results that she later visited the school and added another thousand dollars to the fund. This fund has now assisted about thirty young people.

The Betty Sevier White Memorial Fund

The Betty Sevier White Memorial Fund was established in January, 1919, by her husband, Mr. Henry White, and son, Henry White, Jr., of Jackson, Tennessee. The establishment of this fund is a beautiful and worthy tribute of the one who had been so active in her church life and in her interest in young people.

Lanier Fund

In September, 1920, Mr. W. J. Lanier brought to the President's office $1,500 in bonds, requesting that it be used in assisting worthy students, establishing a fund in memory of father and mother, Mr. and Mrs. J. P. Lanier, and daughter, Rubie Marie. Mr. Lanier has later made additions to his fund. This is a worthy memorial to those who for years were known as among the best friends the students, particularly ministerial students, Union ever had.

W. H. Nichols Fund

In April, 1921, Mr. W. H. Nichols of Kenton, Tennessee, established a fund to be loaned to young ladies studying for missionary work. Mr. Nichols is very much interested in the education of young women for missionaries, and was touched by the fact that while there has been much done for the education of young preachers, there has been no fund of this kind established, so far as the writer knows, to assist missionary girls. It was Mr. Nichols' hope that his establishing this fund would call public attention to the oversight, and that others would join him in an effort to make provision for assisting girls who are offering themselves for missionary work. In this he was not disappointed, for several others have made contributions to this fund.

The L. J. Brooks Fund

In May, 1921, Dr. L. J. Brooks of St. Louis, an alumnus of West Tennessee College, established a fund of $500 in grateful recognition of his interest in his Alma Mater, and in young people, who, as he himself had, have to struggle in getting through college. This fund rendered timely assistance to several worthy students this year.

The Waldrop Brothers Fund

In April, 1922, Messrs. Homer and Floyd Waldrop, students in Union University, realizing the need and value of such funds, upon conditions accepted by the trustees, established a fund of $500—a worthy monument to two worthy students.

Ministerial Loan Fund

The University receives $1,000 annually from the Baptist State Executive Board, which is loaned without interest to young ministers.

Class of 1922

The class of 1922 established a fund of $1,000 as a class memorial. They hope other classes will follow their example, which in the course of a few years would establish sufficient funds to afford every worthy student the opportunity of a college education. There can be no greater testimony to the value of loan funds than the fact that our present student body is so impressed as to establish two such funds themselves this year.

Other Funds

Certain Sunday School classes in the First Baptist Church, Jackson, the Men's Sunday School Class of the First Baptist Church, Clarksville, and the W. M. U. Central Association are laying the foundations of splendid funds which have already made it possible for several of our best students to remain in school this year.

Remarks

The above loan funds are the beginning of what we hope will be a popular movement among our people. This is a peculiar and attractive way in which to invest in young life. It assists, without making dependent, and helps only those who are worthy and ambitious, and since these funds carry a low rate of interest, they will increase through the years. A thousand dollar fund established now, within fifty years will amount to twenty thousand dollars, and in a century will amount to $300,000, after making a liberal deduction for losses.

The writer knew a man in Louisiana who set aside a small sum of money each year to assist some worthy girl through school.

When the writer met him, he had educated eighteen, and since these girls had returned to him the principal and interest, he had a larger fund on hand than when he began. Another man in Kentucky a few years ago placed forty-five dollars in a local bank to pay the tuition of some worthy girl. He soon found such a girl and loaned her the money. She attended a school of which the writer was president, was able to teach the following year, paid back the forty-five dollars and afterwards made her own way through school. The forty-five dollars was loaned to another girl, and in like manner this fund has rendered the assistance needed to make possible the education of six splendid young women, and, two years ago when the writer received this information, the donor still had the original investment in the bank to help another girl that fall. He is so well pleased with the investment that he is now considering increasing it and making it a memorial fund.

The President of Union University will be glad to correspond with anyone interested in establishing such funds.

A Great Memorial

We suggest a great and worthy memorial for someone as follows: A dormitory for girls equipped for the clubbing or light housekeeping plan that has been so successfully in progress here for the last seven years. We have had 300 girls in the history of the club to take advantage of this special boarding plan, and they are all enthusiastic over it. It has enabled many to get an education who could not otherwise have done so. They have reduced the cash cost of their board to an average of $10 a month. We need a large building properly planned and equipped to take care of 100 girls. Such a building would cost forty to fifty thousand dollars. We suggest that the net rents from the building be turned over to a loan fund and be lent out as other funds. This fund would grow under the annual rents and compound interest through the years so that within a century would amount to more than $13,000,000. Other buildings might be erected before the close of that period and thus hundreds of thousands of girls be helped through school. The imagination is staggered at what it would do in the next century—and yet universities stand for a thousand years. This is a great suggestion to somebody.

Rules and Regulations

The above funds, except those specially designated otherwise, are let out under the following regulations: First, funds are available to students who have demonstrated their real worth in school. Class records and deportment in general are considered. They must be recommended by all of their teachers. Second, six per cent interest is charged. Third, at present, owing to the limited amount at our disposal, we must limit the amount loaned any student to one hundred dollars a year. Fourth, students who do not have insurance protection or property must offer approved security.

Form of Will

I, _____, hereby will and bequeath to Union

University _____ to be used as follows:_____

Signed_____

Place and Date_____

Witness_____

Historical Sketch

Union University is the descendant and heir to two earlier institutions: West Tennessee College at Jackson, and Union University at Murfreesboro.

West Tennessee College was established in Jackson about 1842. The early history of the College is almost lost. Only a few fragments remain. It is not definitely known what year the school began or just how it was started or financed. A catalog printed in 1844 has been discovered which gives the faculty and students of the previous year, so that it is known that West Tennessee College was a going concern in 1843. Tradition has it that it was established a few years earlier. However, we will give 1842 as the date of its beginning. The school really had its first conception in the provision of the North Carolina compact in ceding Tennessee to the United States government to be made into a new State. It was provided that there should be three colleges established, one each in East, Middle, and West Tennessee, setting apart certain public lands to that end. But it was not until 1846 that an Act of Congress was passed extinguishing the title to unappropriated lands south and west of the congressional reservation line, and the $40,000 arising from the sale of these lands was set apart as an endowment fund for West Tennessee College, located in Jackson.

The college was chartered in 1846 by an Act of Congress signed by James K. Polk as President of the United States. Hon. Milton Brown represented this district at the time and Andrew Johnson and Jefferson Davis were members of the Congress that passed the enabling Act. The charter was also granted upon the authority of an Act of the Tennessee Legislature, Aaron Brown being Governor. Hon. Harvey Watterson, father of Col. Henry Watterson, being preseident of the Tennessee State Senate, signed the enabling Act. It is rare, indeed, if not without parallel, that an institution of learning should have had as its god-father a President of the United States, an American Congress, a State Governor, and State Legislature, and as afterwards happened, a State Baptist Convention.

Rev. S. M. McKinney, A. M., was first president. Little is known of the details of the development of the school prior to the Civil War. At the close of the war Dr. William Shelton was elected president, and under his administration the school grew rapidly until it was consolidated with Union University in 1873, when the property and endowment was estimated at $90,000.

Among the prominent men educated in West Tennessee College may be named Judge W. B. Turley, father of the United States Senator Turley; Alex W. Campbell and Hon. Wm. H. Jackson, brigadier generals in the Confederate army; Hon. Howell E.

Jackson, United States Supreme Judge; and Judge J. L. H.
Tomlin, Judge Henry W. McCorry, Chancellor E. L. Bullock,
Col. Robert Gates, prominent journalist; Judge Levi Woods,
Rev. A. B. Jones, many years president of M. C. F. I.; Judge
John A. Harrison of St. Louis, Judge Chester G. Bond of Jack-
son, John Williams and Allen Clark, engineers and railroad
builders; Hon. H. C. Anderson, president of the State Senate;
Hon. J. L. Lancaster, receiver Texas & Pacific Railway, Dallas;
Hon. Tom Freeman, receiver for International and Great North-
ern Railway, Dallas; L. J. Brooks of St. Louis, founder and
many years editor of the Jackson Daily Whig, now Jackson Sun;
Hon. H. K. Bryson, late Commissioner of Tenneessee; and a host
of others that have gained national prominence.

In the year 1845 the Baptist General Assembly of Tennessee,
feeling the need of an institution of learning of higher order,
resolved to establish and endow a college known subsequently
as Union University. The proposition had been agitated for
twelve years preceding.

The sum of $65,000 was raised, and the institution was located
at Murfreesboro. The Reverend Dr. Joseph H. Eaton was the
first president, and held this position until death in January,
1859.

During the years from 1861 to 1866, inclusive, the school was
suspended on account of the Civil War. The building was greatly
damaged, the library and apparatus were destroyed, and the endowment was wholly lost.

The school was re-opened in 1866 and continued until 1873,
when an epidemic of cholera and other causes led to a suspension
of all work.

On the 10th day of April, 1874, a convention was called at
Murfreesboro to consider the question of re-establishing a college
for the entire State, and a committee was appointed to locate it.
Among the various propositions presented Jackson was selected
as the best site.

On August 12, 1874, the Tennessee Baptist Convention, then in
session at Trezevant, appointed a Board of Trustees consisting
of thirty-five members. The institution was re-chartered by the
State on June 25, 1875, under the name of the Southwestern Baptist University.

On August 5, 1890, a deed was made to the Southwestern
Baptist University. During this year, Colonel J. W. Rosamon
was chosen as financial agent, and in six months he had a showing of about $30,000 in bonds. During the year 1890 Miss Wil-
lie Edwards, of Shelbyville, Tennessee, made a gift to the endowment fund amounting to $3,310. In November of that year, the
American Baptist Education Society set aside $12,700, $2,700 of
which was to be applied to the payment of the agent's salary to

June 20, 1892; the remaining $10,000 was a gift conditioned on the raising of $40,000 additional to the $30,000 in individual bonds raised by·Col. J. W. Rosamon, as stated above. The same percentage of the $10,000 was paid as that of the $70,000 in individual promises collected in 1897.

In 1897 a movement to endow the Chair of Logic and Moral Philosophy, in honor of Dr. J. R. Graves, resulted in raising $10,000. Dr. H. C. Irby was secretary of the movement.

Through the liberality of Mr. W. T. Adams, of Corinth, Mississippi, a dormitory for young men was erected in 1895, and in 1896 this building was enlarged by the addition of a three-story front. In 1897 a dormitory for young ladies was erected, which, in consequence of a large gift from Mr. J. R. Lovelace, of Martin, Tennessee, was named in honor of his son, Everett Lovelace Hall. Both of these buildings are located on the college campus.

A new chapel was completed in 1899, and, in honor of Dr. W. D. Powell, was named Powell Chapel. In 1901-2 the Perry Estate became the property of the University. With this the Perry School of Bible Instruction was established in memory of Benjamin W. Perry, who gave his estate, amounting to $12,000, requesting it to be used especially in the education of young ministers. In the Spring of 1905, Dr. H. C. Irby gave the University, under conditions accepted by the trustees, $18,000 which, with $7,000 already given, made his gifts amount to $25,000.

In May, 1905, the General Education Society offered the trustees $25,000 on permanent endowment, if the friends of the institution would promptly raise $75,000. The effort securing this offer in 1906 was successful under the leadership of President Hale.

At a meeting of the Board of Trustees, September 17, 1907, the name of the University was changed from Southwestern Baptist University to Union, the name given it in its organization in 1845.

On January 20, 1912, the chapel and main building of the institution were entirely destroyed by fire. Much of the apparatus and the entire library were saved and the loss was partly covered by insurance. A movement to raise funds was immediately set on foot, and, as a result of this movement, the present administration building was erected. On account of liberal gifts of Colonel O. C. Barton, Paris, Tennessee, this building was named in his honor, Barton Hall.

On October 1, 1917, Union University was formally taken over by the United States Government as an army post, in the establishing of a student army training camp, First Lieutenant Ralph Fellows, Commandant—202 students enrolled in the Military Unit.

In January, 1918, a campaign was launched by the Baptists of Tennessee for $100,000 for Union University and most of it subscribed and a part of it paid in cash, when the larger movement, The 75 Million Campaign of Southern Baptists, was launched. Union University's share of this fund is $300,000.

In May, 1922, the citizens of Jackson contributed $30,000 to provide an academy building, gymnasium and other needed improvements.

Union University has had the following presidents:

Jos. H. Eaton guided the initial stages, from the early forties till the formal opening of the College, January, 1848, from then he was president until his death, January 12, 1859; J. M. Pendleton, 1858-61; G. W. Jarman, 1865-71; Charles Manley, 1871-2; Geo. W. Jarman, 1872-90; G. M. Savage, from 1890 to June, 1904; P. T. Hale, 1904-6; G. M. Savage, 1906-7; J. W. Conger, 1907-9; I. B. Tigrett, 1909-11; R. A. Kimbrough, 1911-13; R. M. Inlow was elected June, 1913, but resigned soon after opening of fall term; A. T. Barrett, 1913-15; G. M. Savage, 1915-18; H. E. Watters, 1918-

The longest times of active service as professors were: Jos. H. Eaton, 14 years; Geo. W. Jarman, 40 years; H. C.. Irby, 32 years; T. J. Dupree, 29 years; G. M. Savage, 35 years; A. W. Prince, 15 years.

The College.

The College

ENTRANCE REQUIREMENTS

For admission to the Freshman Class in any regular course leading to a degree, a pupil must offer fifteen units. A unit means a high school course of one scholastic year.

English	3
Mathematics (1½ Alg. and 1 Pl. Geom.)	2½
One Foreign Language	2
History	1
*Science	1
Electives	5½
Total	15

A student deficient in one or more units can make these up in the academy and will not be considered a regular college student until this is done.

* The students in high schools with poor scientific equipment are encouraged to omit science in high school and to spend their time in taking an additional unit in language, English, or history and then to make up their deficiency after they enter Union by electing an extra year of science in college.

WHAT MAY BE OFFERED

TOPICS	Units for A. B.,	SUBJECTS	
English........	3	English Composition and Rhetoric.............	1
		Literature	1
Mathematics...	2	Algebra to Quadratic Equations	1
		Algebra—High School Algebra Completed.....	1
		Plane Geometry	1
History........	1	Ancient History	1
		Modern History	1
		English History	1
		American History and Civics	1
*Latin.........	3	Grammar and Composition, Caesaer, Books I-IV	1
		Six Orations of Cicero	1
		Virgil's Aeneid, First Six Books	1
Greek..........	2	Grammar and Composition	1
		Xenophan's Anabasis, Books I-IV	1
*German.......	1	Elementary Grammar and Reading	1
		Elementary Grammar and Composition........	1
*French........	1	Elementary Grammar and Reading............	1
		Elementary Grammar and Composition........	1
Science........	1	Physiography, with field work................	1
		Experimental Physics	1
		Inorganic Chemistry, with laboratory work....	1
		General Science, with laboratory work........	1
Additional.....		Domestic Science	1
		Domestic Art	1
		Botany, with laboratory work	1
		Zoology, with laboratory work	1
		Agriculture, with laboratory work 1	
		Physiology ....½	
		Bible (If done under accredited teacher and equivalent to a full year of literary work)...	1
		Music (Upon satisfactory examination on at least three year's work)	1
Electives to		Manual Training and Commercial Subjects....	3
Make up		Spanish	1
Total P Units..	15	Military Training or Expression	1

*Entrance units required in Latin or Greek only for the classical group. Two entrance units of a Modern Language required only in the Modern Language Group.

ACCREDITED SCHOOLS

The College desires to promote the growth of thorough secondary schools.

With reference to the relation sustained by the University to academies and high schools, with different courses of study, and different texts, it is difficult to state anything more definite than that the College desires in all cases to give full credit for actual work done, and that certificates from principals, stating the time spent in recitation, the text used, and the parts of books completed in the various courses will be honored, and the student will receive credit for the work equivalent to that in the preparatory department of the College, provided, always, that if the student fails to maintain his standing in the class assigned him, his work in the University is to be the final test of character of previous work.

Advanced College standing will be given on the same conditions as above in case such work has been done with proper equipment and under such conditions as make satisfactory college work possible. No college credit will be given for any work done in high schools.

Credits for advanced standing must be secured by November 15, and must be approved by the heads of the departments concerned.

REQUIREMENTS FOR GRADUATION

The total number of term hours required in each group is 192. Credits are determined by terms; one credit hour means one hour of class work a week in a single subject throughout a term. The school year is divided into three terms, so that the above requirement is equivalent to 64 year hours or 128 semester hours.

In each group a certain number of electives may be taken from any of the regular college courses offered, but must be other than those required in that particular group. However, the wise student will always finish his required work first. Failure to do this frequently forces students to do more than 192 hours in order to graduate.

Credit for work done in the Fine Arts departments can be counted only when not also counted toward graduation in those departments.

Remarks:

CLASSIFICATION

College students will be classified as follows:

(a) A student will be classified as a Freshman who has no conditions required for entrance and is carrying at least 12 hours of Freshman work in the Fall Term.

(b) A student will be classified as a Sophomore who has no condition required for entrance and at the beginning of the Fall or Winter Term has at least 36 hours of College work to his credit.

(c) A student will be classified as a Junior who has no condition for entrance, and who, at the beginning of the Fall Term has at least 90 hours to his credit.

(d) A student will be classified as a Senior who at the beginning of the Fall Term has at least 138 hours to his credit.

Note: Nothing in these requirements may prevent a student's

changing to a higher class the last term of the year, provided he
has made up his deficiencies by that time.

The University at present is offering but three degrees: Bachelor of Arts, Bachelor of Science, and Bachelor of Music. The
requirements for the Bachelor of Arts degree are indicated in the
chart on the opposite page, and in the remarks following on the
next page.

For the Bachelor of Science degree the student may substitute
Education or Science for the two years of foreign language in
Groups III and IV. The requirements for the two degrees, B. S.
and A. B., are otherwise the same.

For the degree of Bachelor of Music, students must meet the
regular college entrance requirements, and present 192 hours of
college work, including the regular course prescribed in music.

128 semester hours.

GROUP I. Classical	GROUP II. Biblical	GROUP III. Modern Language or Science	GROUP IV. Sociological-Educational
Freshman Year— Hrs.	**Freshman Year—** Hrs.	**Freshman Year—** Hrs.	**Freshman Year—** Hrs.
English 12	English 12	English 12	English 12
Mathematics 12	Mathematics 12	Mathematics 12	Mathematics 12
*Latin 9	*Latin 9	*Modern Lang. 9	*Foreign Lang. 9
*Greek 9	*Greek 9	Chemistry 12	Chemistry 12
Bible (Old Test.) ..8	Bible (Old Test.) ..8	Bible (Old Test.) ..6	Bible (New Test.) ..6
Sophomore Year— Hrs.	**Sophomore Year—** Hrs.	**Sophomore Year—** Hrs.	**Sophomore Year—** Hrs.
English 9	English 9	English 9	English 9
Latin 9	Greek 9	Mh. or Science 9	Foreign Lang. 9
Greek 9	Chemistry 12	Two Md. Lang. 18	(Same as above)
Chemistry 12	Sociology 9	or Biol. and Phys...18	Sociology 9
Sociology 9	Bible (New Test.) ..6	Old Test 2	Old Te t. 2
Bible (New Test.) ..6	Electives 4	Bible (New Test.) ..6	Education 9
Electives 4		... 4	Ble (New Te t.) ...6
			Electives 4
Junior Year— Hrs.	**Junior Year—** Hrs.	**Junior Year—** Hrs.	**Junior Year—** Hrs.
History 9	History 9	History 9	History 9
Polit. Sc. or Economics, 6	Polit. Sc. or Economics, 6	Polit. Sc. or Economics, 6	Polit. Sc. or Economics, 6
Psychology 6	Psychol gy 6	Psychology 6	Psychology 6
Biology 9	New Test. Gr. 9	Adv., Lab. Sci. or Mod.	Education or
Glogy 6	...	Lang. or Mathematics 9	Sociology 9
Electives 12	Electives 12	Electives 16	Electives 14
Senior Year— Hrs.	**Senior Year—** Hrs.	**Senior Year—** Hrs.	**Senior Year—** Hrs.
Logic 4	Logic 4	Logic 4	Logic 4
Ethics 4	Ethics 4	Ethics 4	Ethics 4
Sociology 9	Education 9	Sociology 9	Education or
Electives 28	Electives 28	Electives 28	Sociology 9
			Electives 28

REMARKS.—It will be noted that the above groups are really six in number, namely: Classical, Biblical, Modern Language, Scientific, Sociological, and Educational, and in other departments two others are provided: Agriculture and Music. It will also be observed that these courses conform pretty closely to the Major and Minor systems used in many schools. Anyone desiring to major in any other subjects, as English, Greek, or History, will see the head of that department who in conference with the Dean and President, will suggest suitable modifications of one of the above groups to give a properly balanced course. Usually, however, it will only be necessary for one to elect additional twelve to eighteen hours in his major subject, in the nearest related group. For example, to major in Greek or Latin, one would elect the additional hours in Latin or Greek in Group I in his Junior and Senior years; in English, he would simply elect English in Groups I or II in his Junior and Senior years. To major in History he would simply elect two extra years of History in Group IV.

*In the classical group the student must present four years of Latin or Greek or of both as entrance credit, or else elect enough college hours in these subjects to make up the deficit.

In Group II if three years of Latin are presented for entrance credit, no more Latin will be required. If no Latin is presented, candidate must take two years of Latin in this Group.

Two years of some modern language must be presented for entrance credit in the Modern Language group. If student majors in Foreign Language, candidate must take not less than two years in the same language presented for entrance, and two or more years of some other modern language.

It is earnestly recommended that every student take at least 27 hours in each of two departments.

Graduating thesis must be handed in to Committee not later than May 1st preceding graduation. Subject must be approved by the Committee.

No one will be considered a member of the Senior Class until passed upon by the faculty in session. All conditions must be removed by the opening of the last term. No one with conditions may have his name appear on the class announcements without special permission from the faculty. Those who enter their last term with no conditions may be excused from final examinations provided they have been faithful in their work and make "excellent" on their daily grades for the term. This rule does not apply to Freshmen subjects taken in the Senior year, nor does it exempt in the Spring term those who are to graduate in the Summer term.

No student may receive a degree who has not had at least three terms in residence.

Students may have two bachelor degrees (e. g. Bachelor of Arts and Bachelor of Music) conferred when the requirements of both have been fully met, provided that he has not less than forty hours to offer over and above that required for the first degree.

AUGUST COMMENCEMENT

The Summer School has so grown in importance that it has become necessary to hold a convocation at the close to confer degrees upon those who finish at that time. Such students are counted with and considered a part of the Senior class going out in the regular spring convocation.

Department of Agriculture

DR. DAVIS, Dean

PROF. DUNN
PROF. PRINCE

PROF. HUDSON
PROF. M. DAVIS

Agriculture is America's greatest business. More money is invested and more people engaged in this than that of any other business, and yet the vast majority of those engaged in it have had no special training for it. Imagine a doctor, lawyer, teacher, or bookkeeper succeeding today without special training. The farmer's business is the most intricate, the nature of his problems the most complex, the elements which he must deal with the most varied of all businesses or professions, and in none does special technical training yield greater returns. Few sections of the world are more favorably situated for diversified farming than is West Tennessee. Union University, located in the very heart of West Tennessee, offers thorough and practical training in a wide variety of courses. For those who desire to take full four years of technical training in agriculture, we would recommend that they take only two or at the most three years with us and then finish in some agricultural college. Those who want a well-rounded, literary education for the farm, or other business, will do well to elect a few courses from each of the four departments we offer, Agronomy, Animal Husbandry, Dairy Husbandry, and Horticulture.

Union University is favorably located for the teaching of Agriculture. The West Tennessee Experiment Station and Demonstration Farm is located here, and the students of Union will be accorded the fullest possible opportunity for observing scientific agriculture, horticulture and dairying in actual practice. The students will have opportunity to do some practical experiments of their own. The farm is in charge of Mr. A. S. Roberts, one of the best scientific farmers in West Tennessee, who is in thorough sympathy with the agricultural department of Union University, and will render every assistance possible. The University, therefore, has at its disposal a plant which it could not reproduce and operate for less than two hundred thousand dollars.

In addition to the above, members of the faculty operate a large farm and a fine orchard, where students may have practical observation.

An experienced and highly qualified man is in charge of this department. There is perhaps not a better qualified man in Tennessee than Dr. Davis.

AGRICULTURAL GROUP

Freshman Year

English I, II, III .... (1, 2)
Mathematics .... (1c)
Physics .... (2b)
Field Crops I, II (F. & W.) .... (1)
Animal Husbandry I (S) .... (2)
Biology I, II, III (F. W. S.) .... (1, 2)
Chemistry I, II, III (F. W. S.) .... (1. 2)
Physical Training and Hygiene .... (1, 2)

Sophomore Year

Chemistry IV, VI, VIII .... (3a, 4a)
Botany IV, V (F. & W.) .... (4)
Bacteriology VI (S.) .... (3a)
Zoology (Heredity) VII (S.) .... (3)
Geology I, II (F. & W.) .... (4)
Dairying I, II (F. & W.) .... (3)
Horticulture I (S.) .... (4)
Economics .... (5)
Animal Husbandry II, III (F. & W.) .... (4a)
Physics .... (3b)
Soils I, II .... (4a)

Note: Parenthetical figures refer to courses in the University of Tennessee catalog.

AGRONOMY

AGRONOMY 1. *Soils.*—In this is given an interesting and practical presentment of the origin, formation and classification of soils, their physical properties, mechanical composition, relation to water, air, and heat; the principles and methods of tillage; the principles of drainage and its effects upon moisture supply. temperature, aeration, chemical and biological activity; drouth resistence, and general productiveness of soils; the physical improvement of soils, etc. Sophomore Fall term. Two hours.

Everyone who ever expects to have anything to do with farming or gardening should take this course.

AGR. I. (a) *Soil Physics.*—This is a laboratory course dealing with the principles of soils involved in Agronomy I. Sophomore Fall and Winter term. One two-hour period.

AGR. II. *Soils.*—This course deals with some special properties of soil relation to moisture, air, and heat. Special attention to the work of experiment stations. Sophomore Winter term. Two hours.

AGR. III. *Soil Fertility.*—This is an interesting study of the sources, properties, and relative values of the more important commercial fertilizing materials; the utilization of farm manure, forms, properties and use of lime; the maintenance of organic matter in the soil, and the general up-building of fertility. Elective Spring term. Two hours.

FIELD CROPS

In this the student studies the characteristics, adaptations, culture, and use of most important grain and forage crops, and the principles of crop rotation, with their application under various conditions. The course is divided into two parts:

FIELD CROPS I. *Grain Crops.*—Fall term. Two hours recitation and one two-hour laboratory period. For Freshmen.

FIELD CROPS II. *Forage Crops.*—Winter term. Two hours recitation and one two-hour laboratory period. For Freshmen.

ANIMAL HUSBANDRY

ANIMAL HUSBANDRY I.—*Live-Stock Judging.*—Scoring of individuals and judging of groups representing the more common classes of swine, sheep, and dairy cattle from the standpoint of the market and the producer. Freshman. Spring term. Three hours.

A. H. II.—*Breeds of Stock.*—Lectures and text on the origin, history, utility, adaptability, characteristics, conformation and management of the various races of domestic animals. Sophomore. Fall term. Three hours.

A. H. III.—*Live-stock Management.*—A detailed study of the practical methods and principles involved in the feeding, breeding and management of all classes of live stock. The laboratory work consists of demonstrations and exercises in the growing and handling of grade and pedigreed stock. Sophomore Winter term. Two hours and one laboratory period.

DAIRY HUSBANDRY

DAIRYING I. *Elements of Dairying.*—A general survey of dairying and its relation to agriculture; secretion and composition and properties of milk; effect of breed, period of lactation, age and feed on the quantity and quality of milk; study of the Babcock test, the lactometer; methods of creaming, farm separators; care of milk and cream on the farm, causes of souring. Sophomore. Fall term. Two recitations and one two-hour laboratory period.

DAIRYING II. *Testing of Dairy Products.*—Must be preceded by Dairying I. Commercial methods of determining fat, salt, moisture, acidity, caesin, total solids, and solids not fat in milk and its products; standardization of milk, cream, alkaline solutions and acid, detection of adulterants and preservations; quality test of milk. Sophomore. Winter test. Three hours. Two-thirds of time given to laboratory work.

DAIRYING III. *Creamery Butter Making and Factory Management.*—The theory and practice of factory buttermaking, sampling and grading of milk and cream; cream ripening, starters, pasteurization; factory management; factory construction; churning; marketing; butter scoring.

This is largely a laboratory course. Elective. Spring term. Three hours.

HORTICULTURE

HORTICULTURE I. *Principles of Fruit Growing.*—This course treats of the principles of plant propagation, care and management of small plantations of tree fruits and small fruits, reclamation of old orchards, and the application of control measures for insects and diseases affecting the common fruits. Elective. Sophomore. Fall term. Three hours.

HORTICULTURE II. *Principles of Vegetable Growing.*—A general survey is made of the vegetable crops; garden rotations, varieties and management of vegetable crops; garden rotations, companion and succession cropping and the making and care of hot beds, and cold frames, with special emphasis on the Farmer's Home Garden. Elective. Sophomore. Winter term. Three hours.

HORTICULTURE III. *Practice in Horticulture.*—This is a laboratory course in plant propagation, with emphasis on layering, grafting, budding, pruning; making of spraying material and the actual application of same in the orchard. Elective. Sophomore. Spring term. Three hours.

HORTICULTURE IV. *Landscape Gardening.*—The principles of landscape gardening are studied with special reference in laying out and planting home and school grounds. The student becomes acquainted with the ornamental trees, shrubs and vines and the proper use of each in landscape work. Elective for those who have had Biology IV. Spring term. Three hours.

REMARK.—Certainly every teacher and every home-maker should take this course. What a beautiful country this could be made by properly banking with shrubs and flowers every home, school, church and public building! Bible.

Bible

Fourteen hours of Bible are required of all graduates. Students may elect to take this in any of the courses offered, but they should be so elected as to cover both Old and New Testaments. Since Bible is required of non-theological students, many of whom are of various religious faiths, and since Union University desires scrupulously to respect the individual religious feelings and previous training of each student, a special Bible course is provided that will be in the strictest sense non-sectarian. Those who wish to take a Bible course interpreted from the Baptist standpoint will elect some of the classes offered in the Theological Department, for which college credit will be given.

OLD TESTAMENT

DR. SAVAGE

A course of three terms is offered, two hours each term. This is an inductive study of the plain unannotated Bible text without helps. An effort is made to get at just what the plain English text seems to mean when studied as any other literary book. The object is to get a practical and comprehensive view of the historical facts and the meaning of the poetical and prophetical books when studied as literary productions.

The teacher reads the Old Testament in the Hebrew, also the Septuagir, and has traveled over much of the country referred to in the Scriptures. He uses a large raised map of the Holy Land which, together with the fresh illustrations and explanations from the teacher's personal observation, adds much interest to the study.

These are listed as Courses Bible I, II, and III. Six hours.

NEW TESTAMENT

DR. MANTEY

Three terms of two hours each will be devoted to a study of the New Testament. The aim will be to secure as complete knowledge as is possible in the time of the historical and literary content of the various parts of the New Testament. Considerable attention will be given to the study of the environment of early Christianity, distinctive customs of the Jews, idiomatic expressions, occasions of production, date of writing, etc. This is a comprehensive survey course covering all the New Testament, designed to give the student an intelligent, historical, and reverent conception of Christianity.

The entire New Testament is covered during the year. The courses are listed as Bible IV, V, VI. Two hours each.

Three additional courses are offered in New Testament epistles. Two hours a week, elective for Seniors.

This is a study of the New Testament Epistles for their historical, social, and religious teachings, without a discussion of those questions which are involved in the denominational differences of the members of the class. The aim being to give a general knowledge of these writings without anything that could be construed into an attempt to proselyte non-Baptist students.

The date, authorship, circumstance of production, literary character, and general outline of each will be studied.

These courses are listed as Bible VII, VIII, IX. Two hours each.

For other courses in Bible, see Department of Theology.

Department of Education

DR. HOGAN
PROF. RUTLEDGE

The aim of the whole educational system has changed most radically in recent years; from the individual to the social viewpoint; from the informational to the developmental; from education for education's sake to education for service's sake. It is the purpose of the Department of Education to make its contribution towards this end. This will be done in the selection of text books, in the planning of the courses, in the methods used, and in the suggestions and inspiration of the teacher. The aim will be to have socialized texts, socialized courses, socialized methods, and socialized students.

It is also the aim of the Department to meet the demand of the educational laws of Tennessee and the adjoining states,—and, also, to raise the standard for teachers by impressing the students with the sacred aim of the profssion. This will dignify the work, and hence command larger appropriation, better equipment and increased salaries.

Normal Courses

The Normal Course, as will be observed, is only a slight modification of the regular Freshman and Sophomore years of College. Those completing it may receive a Normal Diploma upon which the State Department of Education will issue a high school certificate valid to teach in any second and third class school in Tennessee. This is the same certificate that is issued upon a diploma from the State Normal Schools.

First Year	Hrs.	*Second Year*	Hrs.
English	12	English	9
Mathematics	9	Foreign Language	9
Foreign Language	9	Sociology	9
Some Natural Science	9	History	9
Education	9	Education	9
Bible	6	Bible	6

Degree Course

This course consists of the regular four-year College course leading to A. B. or B. S. degrees, in which the student must elect a minimum of twenty-seven hours of Education from the courses outlined below. Those receiving this degree are entitled to receive first-class high school certificate from the State of Tennes- and a high school certificate will be issued upon this degree in practically all the States in the Union.

ED. I. *Elementary Psychology.* Elective for Freshmen.— Three hours a week for the first quarter. The attempt is to give students a working grasp of the more important basis of understanding the mental background to human behavior. Constant reference is made to applying the ideas developed to teaching situations. Reading, Reports, Discussions, Notes.

ED. II. *Modern Elementary Methods.* Open to all classes. Three hours per week second quarter. Since development is the educational aim, th pupils should be taught to think. To this end the sociology methods will be used; also the problem and the proper methods; molivation of pupils involving interest and effort.

There will be observation teaching, and practice teaching.

Readings, Reports, Discussions, Notes.

ED. III. *Modern Secondary School Methods.* The same general methods outlined in Course II will be used in advanced form and made to apply to students in the Junior High and the High School. Open to all classes. Three hours per week for third quarter.

Readings, Reports, Discussions, Notes.

ED. IV. *Introductory Study of Rural Education.*—Analysis of rural life in the United States today; a study of the place of the public school in the rural life. Elective for Sophomores.

Three hours a week, third quarter. Readings, Reports, Discussions, Notes.

Text: Cubberley, Rural Life and Education.

ED. V. *School and Class Room Management.*—Elective for Sophomores, Juniors and Seniors. Consideration of the teacher, school buildings, equipment, curriculum, assigning of lessons, the recitation, etc., as related to school government, discipline. Three hours a week, second quarter.

Text: Bagley, School Room Management.

ED. VI. *Methods of Study and Methods of Teaching.*—Elective for Juniors and Seniors. This course will deal largely with the motives that should prompt students to study; also the methods of teaching, bringing into play the fundamental principles of education. Reading, Reports, Discussions, Notes. Three hours a week, third quarter.

Texts: McMurry; Strayer, How to Teach.

ED. VII. *Public School Administration.*—Elective for Sophomores, Juniors and Seniors. This course deals with the outer aspects of the subject, such as school laws, organizations, finance, buildings, equipment, and supervision. Readings, Reports, Discussions, Notes. Three hours a week, third quarter.

Text: Cubberley, Public School Administration.

ED. VIII. *History of Education.*—Elective for Freshmen and Sophomores. The aim of this course is to give students a sufficient knowledge of the development of educational thought to enable them to see why our education systems are as they are and where, and how one has to attach present-day problems. Readings, Reports, Discussions, Notes. Three hours a week, third quarter.

Text: Monro's Brief Course.

ED. IX. *General Psychology.*—Required of A. B. students. Elective for Sophomores, Juniors and Seniors. The study of the nervous system as it is related to the mind. The fundamental principles of Psychology are discussed, dealing with the biological and social inheritances, and also the S. R. Bond System. It will lay a deep and broad foundation for all activities of life. Three hours a week first quarter.

ED. X. *Educational Psychology.*—Elective for all students except Freshmen. Prerequisite: General or Elementary Psychology. This course will deal with the learning process, giving a careful study of instinct, interest and effort, concepts, precepts, transfer of training, S. R. Bond System, mental processes and moral training as related to the growth of the child's mind. Read-

•

ings, Reports, Discussions, Notes. Three hours a week, second quarter.

ED. XI. *Philosophy of Education.*—Open to Seniors. This course will deal with the basic principles that underlie the general educational system, with discussions related to the educational standards and methods, together with the analysis of the process of the acquisition of knowledge. Readings, Reports, Discussions. Three hours a week, third quarter.

Text: Horne's Philosophy of Education.

ED. XII. *Genetic Psychology.*—Elective for all except Freshmen. A study of the theory of mental development and some of the phases of mental genesis representative in childhood, adolescence and maturity; and the application of the psychological methods to the problems and practical interests of life. Readings, Reports, Discussions, Notes. Three hours a week, third quarter.

Text: Kirkpatrick, Genetic Psychology.

ED. XIII. *School Hygiene.*—Elective for Seniors. This course will deal with medical inspection, school-room lighting and ventilation, the hygiene of instruction, etc. These and related topics make up the basis of discussion. Readings, Reports, Discussions, Notes. Three hours a week, second quarter.

Text: Dressler, School Hygiene.

Texts: Dressler's School Hygiene, and Rutledge's Course and Diploma Course.

ED. XIV. . *Public School Problems.*—This course is open to students with over 100 college hours or to correspondence students who are actually engaged in public school teaching. Four hours.

Topie: Classification, Promotion, Acceleration, Retardation, etc.

ED. XV. *Tests and Measurements.*—This course deals with the common statistical methods used in school measurements and the several measurements in the various subjects of the curriculum of the elementary schools and of the curriculum of the high schools. The literature on the subject reviewed. Aim of the course is to enable teachers to test their schools scientifically.

Text: Monro's, Educational Tests and Measurements.

ED. XVI. *Social Education.*—Open to Freshmen and Sophomores. The course will have to do with informal education and indirect teaching, linking up the life of the child in the home, the church and the community with the work done in the school. It will take up the Sociological School, Curriculum, Methods and

Discipline. Readings, Reports, Discussions, Notes.. Three hours per week, first quarter.

ED. XVII. *Social Psychology.*—Open to Juniors and Seniors. This course will follow Courses I and X, and its purpose will be to lay a foundation for the course—The Social Principles of Education. It will deal with the viewpoint of *the plain* and *the current;* differentiation and initiation, and the individual and the group assembly. Three hours per week, second quarter.

ED. XVIII. *The Principles of Secondary Education.*—Open to all students. This is a very comprehensive course. It will study the Secondary Schools of America and other countries; the relation of the Elementary School with the High School; the program of studies and school organization. Three hours per week, third quarter.

ED. XIX. *The School System of Tennessee.*—Open to all classes. This will be an original course, studying the school situation of the State first-hand. Its merits and demerits will be examined, and suggestions will be made for improvement. Papers, Questionnaires, Discussions, Notes. Two hours per week.

REMARK.—Arrangements have been made with the splendid city schools of Jackson, C. B. Ijams, Superintendent, for ample observation. A splendid grammar school adjoining the campus under the principalship of M. M. Summar is especially convenient and helpful.

Department of English

DR. SHANKLE

REMARK.—We do not offer at any one time nor in any one year all of the courses listed in any department.

The instruction given in English has three objects in view: First, a command of correct and clear English, spoken and written; second, the power of accurate and intelligent reading and the development of the habit of reading good literature with appreciation and enjoyment; third, a knowledge of certain authors whose work illustrate the development, not only of the English language, but aso of the English literature. Etymology and Philologywill receive sufficient attention to enable the student to understand the formation, growth and development of the English language from the beginning to the present time. Correct spelling and grammatical accuracy will be rigorously exacted in connection with all written work during the entire course. *Students notably deficient in spelling, reading, and English Grammar will be required to make this up before entering the senior year.*

In addition to the class work, themes and reports on parallel reading are required. Parallel reading for each term is announced at the beginning of the term. This work will be made both interesting and helpful. Many themes on popular subjects will be assigned so the student's work may render him or her a happy service later in public, religious or social services.

A Bonus for Good Mother Tongue.

As a special stimulant for good English, the faculty has decided to give an extra plus to all term grades or standings in all subjects for extra good spelling, pennmanship, and clear, forceful, graceful English, or a like discount for the lack of it.

ENGLISH I. *Freshman Composition.*—This course is conducted by means of lectures, quizzes, papers, reports, and in addition to this a text book for class use. Special emphasis will be placed on the infinitive, participle, all verb formations, sentence structure, the rules of syntax, and growth and development of the language.

Text used, Genung's Working Principles of Rhetoric and an Outline of Grammar by the Professor in charge, and Payne's "Learning to Spell." Four hours.

ENG. II. *Composition.*—This course will include a review of the formal elements of composition, such as punctuation, capitalization, sentence-structure and paragraph-structure. Daily short themes and longer weekly themes on subjects taken from the student's own observation and experience will be required. The various types of composition—exposition, description, narration, argumentation—will be discussed and theme practice in the different types will be required. Especial attention will be given to note taking. Four hours.

ENG. III. *Mythology.*—Myths of Greece and Rome, together with those of other nations, are studied as to development, interpretation and relation to literature and art. Weekly theses will be required in addition to the class work. Four hours.

ENG. IV.—*American Literature.*—In this course special attention will be given to American life and culture, and to the study of the New England and the Southern group of writers in order to reach a better understanding of the intellectual and social tendencies of the two sections. Besides the text book there will be essays, lectures, and quizzes. The first term's work will be given to American Prose, and the last two terms' work will be given to the study of American Poetry. The courses will be numbered IV (a), IV (b) and IV (c).

Texts used: Page's Chief American Poets, Alden's Introduction to Poetry and some good anthology of American Prose. Crabb's English Synonyms. Three hours.

ENG. V. *Shakespeare.*—Critical and textual study of four or more of Shakespeare's best plays. Rolft's edition recommended. Plays to be studied in class: Hamlet, Macbeth, King Lear, Othello, and Henry VIII. Three hours.

ENG. VI. *a. Milton.*—A general consideration of Milton as a whole with special study of the longer poems including Comus, Samson Agonistes, and Paradise Lost.
b. Dante.—A critical study of "The Divine Comedy" will be made in this course.

ENG. VII. *Tennyson.*—This course will include the reading and writing of critiques on the Idyls of the King, Timbuctoo, The Princess, In Memoriam, The Holy Grail, and such other poems as the time will permit. A careful study of the life of Tennyson will be made. Three hours.

ENG. VIII. *Browning.*—This course includes a close study of the life of Browning and a careful analysis will be made of Men and Women, The Ring and the Book, Saul, Pippa Passes, and such other poems as the teacher and the class may select. A critique will be required on each poem read. Course open to seniors. Texts: Browning's Complete Poems, and Claybrook's Thesis: How Browning's Poetry Contributes to Social Development. Three hours.

ENG. IX. *The Novel.*—Cross's Development of the English Novel and Pery's Study of Prose Fiction are used as guides. The historical and critical teaching of these books will be applied in the analysis of representative novels and short stories from Henry Fielding to our own time. Open to seniors. Three hours.

ENG. X. *The Novel.*—One or more novels from Scott, Dickens, George Elliot, or Thackery is read and a critique is written upon the novel read. Course open to seniors. Three to four hours.

ENG. XI. *Advanced Theme Writing.*—The aim of this course is to teach correctness and clearness in the expression of thought, and to stimulate the powers of observation, imagination, and reflection in the student. Sixteen themes on assigned topics are required of the student during the term, and daily work in meaning, origin, derivation, and pronunciation of words as found in some standard dictionary is required. Open to juniors and seniors. Three or five hours.

ENG. XII. *Science of Construction.*—The purpose of this course is to give a thorough knowledge of the fundamental principles of the grammar of the English language. Both technical and formal grammar will be stressed. The student will be taught to see the connection between grammar and thinking. Our grammar is what it is because our thinking is what it is. Along with this course there will be a number of parallel readings and research work from the leading grammarians of the present time. Course required of those who show a deficiency in the fundamentals. Four hours.

ENG. XIII. *Theory of Composition.*—The purpose of this course is to train the student to write correctly and clearly about the things he already knows; to use reference books, and to take notes.

Course open to all who have failed to get a hold on this subject before coming to College. Three hours.

REMARK.—A special drill and study class in debating will be conducted throughout the year, from which speakers will be selected to participate in the inter-collegiate debates referred to on another page. Proper credit in English will be given for work done in this class.

Department of French

DR. SAVAGE

French has rapidly grown in popularity since the war and is one of the few foreign languages that High School and College students now want to speak. It is one of the most beautiful of spoken languages and yet one of the most difficult for English tongues to speak correctly. Union University is fortunate in this department in having at its head, not only a great scholar who has been teaching the language for years, and one who has studied it in Paris, and speaks it correctly, but he is ably and fortunately assisted by Madam Damaris Muller, a native French lady who assists very materially in aiding students to acquire the spoken language, and further guarantees that the pronunciation and accent will be correct. It also adds a fine interest and confidence in the classes.

A splendid compliment was paid this department last year in that a graduate of the year before class, Miss Marie Rutledge, was awarded a scholarship in one of the colleges of France. There were twenty scholarships awarded in America and only two of them came to Southern students. In the awarding of these scholarships, the character of the training in French was given great consideration.

FRENCH I, II, III.—Fall, Winter and Spring terms. Composition, dictation and reading of easy stories and history, as Lamartine's *Scenes de la Revolution Francaise.* The pronunciation of French this year is particularly emphasized. As rapidly as a class can bear it, instruction is given by using the French language. Nine hours.

Text: The New Fraser and Squaire French Grammar.

FRENCH LITERATURE

FRENCH IV, V, VI.—Throughout the fall, winter and spring terms. The class here will be better able to use French terms in giving rules of grammar and composition. After reading selected works of Chateaubriend, Voltaire, Racine, etc., the remainder of the lessons will be occupied with stories of the nineteenth century writers. Nine hours.

Text: Carnahan's Short French Review Grammar.

ADVANCED FRENCH LITERATURE

FRENCH VIII, IX.—Winter and spring terms. Conversation still more exclusively in French. The reading this year will be chiefly of writers of the seventeenth century—Moliere, Boileau, and others. Six hours.

In view of present conditions, an hour will be given every day to such as are eager to have a speaking knowledge of the French language. Conversations on various subjects.

FRENCH X, XI, XII.—French composition, toether with a study of the philosophy of the language and critical study of some of the best literature. Nine hours.

FRENCH XIII, XIV, XV.—A continuation of French IV, studying especially poetry and philosophy. Nine hours.

Department of Greek

DR. MANTEY

A recent graduate of Union who is studying medicine now, said that he regrets that he did not study Greek while in Union, because so many medical terms are derived from the Green language. The same can be said about scores of words used in other professions. But certainly every one entering the ministry, if he has as much as average ability, should by all means study Greek so as to know first-hand the teachings of the New Testament.

GREEK I. *Beginners.*—Fall term. Three hours.

GREEK II. *Beginners.*—Winter term. Three hours. Continuation of Greek I.

GREEK III. *Beginners,*—Spring term. Three hours. Continuation of Greek II.

Prerequisites, two units of Latin. The class begins with the Greek alphabet and spends the entire session on the elements of the language, with daily translations of Greek into English and English into Greek. Special attention given to form, construction and the fundamentals of Syntax. College credit given unless offered for entrance.
Text: Benner & Smith, *"Beginners' Greek Book."*

GREEK IV. *Xenophon's "Anabasis" and Greek Grammar.*—Fall term. Three hours.

GREEK V. *Xenophon's "Anabasis" and Greek Grammar.*—Winter term. Three hours. Continuation of Greek IV.

GREEK VI. *Xenophon's "Anabasis" and Greek Grammar.*—Spring term. Three hours. Continuation of Greek V.
This course consists of two parts:

(1) Reading in the "Anabasis." An effort will be made to read four books, but if necessary for thoroughness a smaller amount will be covered. The student is questioned as to forms and constructions, and the meaning of particular words. Side lights are sought by the requirement of parallel readings in the lives of Xenophon, Cyrus the Elder, Cyrus the Younger, and the reading, in translation, of at least one volume of the "Cyropaedia," with written reviews of the parallel readings and the progress of the expedition is traced on the map.
Text: Goodwin and White.

(2) *Grammar and Composition.* Text: Goodwin's Greek Grammar. The Grammar will be studied from the beginning

through "Formation of Words," of a solid foundation for the study of Syntax in the following year. Written translations of English into Greek will be required regularly, and the development of words from roots as set forth in the supplement to the text of the Anabasis will be carefully studied.

GREEK VIII. *New Testament.*—Selections from the Gospel and Grammar. Fall term. Three hours.

GREEK VIII. *New Testament.*—Selections from Pauline Epistles, and Grammar. Winter term. Three hours.

GREEK IX. *New Testament.*—Selections from Hebrews, Peter, and Revelation, and Grammar. Spring term. Three hours.

The aim is (1) to give the student such an acquaintance with the various types of Greek in the New Testament and with the *Koine* in general, that he may profitably pursue its study by himself; (2) To study selected passages illustrative of the types of Greek in the New Testament, which will be studied intensively according to the principles of interpretation, and which will prove helpful in doing Christian work.

"A Manual of The Greek New Testament," by Dana and Mantey, will be used as a guide for the grammar lessons.

GREEK X. *New Testament.*—Acts. Fall term. Three hours.

GREEK XI. *New Testament.*—Acts. Winter term. Three hours.

GREEK XII. *New Testament.*—Acts will be completed, and if there is time one of the shorter epistles will be studied. Spring term. Three hours.

These courses alternate with VII., VIII., IX., and will be open to those who have completed Greek VI.

A careful study will be made of the language with special attention to the etymology of words, to forms, and to construetions. Robertson's "Grammar of the Greek New Testament" will be used constantly for reference.

These courses will also be open to those who prefer to take their fourth year Greek in the New Testament rather than in Classical Greek. These students will be expected to do research work on the usage of important words, and make exegeses of certain passages.

The J. R. Graves Society offers a medal to the student making the highest grade in the fourth year Greek. This will apply whether the fourth year is taken in New Testament or Classical Greek.

Department of History and Political Science

PROF. RUTLEDGE

History, Economics, and Political Science are inseparably connected. History is largely the record of the economic and political changes and conditions of man. The chief problems before man today, as in all the past, are economic and social. These make up the leading political questions. Therefore every citizen to vote, talk or act intelligently must know something of the great underlying principles of these great subjects. This is the purpose of all the courses in this department.

ECONOMICS I, II, III. Three two-hour courses cover the field of Economics in a comprehensive manner which lays the foundation for an intelligent life-long study of these problems as they shall be discussed in the press, platform, pulpit, and the street corner in future years.

POLITICAL SCIENCE I, II, III. Three two-hour courses in the Science of Government, including comprehensive study of European Government and an intensive study of the American Constitution.

HISTORY

HIST. I. Modern Europe from 1600 to 1789. Special stress · will be placed on the Reformation, Divine Monarchy. Credit 3 hours.

HIST. II. This course emphasizes the French Revolution, the Napoleonic campaigns, the Era of Mettennich, The Industrial Revolution, and The Growth of Nationalism. Credit 3 hours.

HIST. III. This course is a continuation of Course II. It calls special attention to the unification of Germany and Italy and to the development of European countries under modern conditions. Attention is given to national imperialism. Credit 3 hours.

HIST. IV. English History. A study of the origin and growth of the English people; the development of the institutional life; their economic life; the Magna Chartar, etc. Credit 3 hours.

HIST. V. A continuation of Course IV. Special emphasis will be placed on the Tudor Despotism; rise of parliament and the development of the English Constitution. Credit 3 hours.

HIST. V. English History completed. Stress will be placed upon English imperialism. Credit 3 hours.

HIST. VI. American History Topics: Explorations and discoveries; settlements and colonial development; Revolutionary period to the adoption of the Constitution. Prerequisite: English History. Credit 3 hours.

HIST. VII. A continuation of Course VI. Special attention is given to the rise and interplay of sectional forces and the part played by the South in national history, the problems of the Civil War.

HIST. VIII. In this course the Reconstruction period is carefully examined. Special attention is given to recent history. Credit 3 hours.

Department of Home Economics

MISS CHARLOTTE H. WATSON, *Director*

MISS GRACE POWERS, MISS CLAIR GILBERT,
Assistants

This department has been growing in interest and popularity until it has entirely outgrown its quarters. New quarters have been provided. A complete suite of rooms consisting of domestic science room, serving room, fitting room, and domestic art room, four rooms in all, have been provided and equipped. The teacher in charge is well trained, thorough, and well equipped to develop a strong department. Special attention will be given to training teachers in Domestic Science and Domestic Art.

Purpose

The teaching of Home Economics has a three-fold aim, material, social, and ethical.

Material Aim: To teach the fundamental lessons in cooking and sewing; the basic principles of housewifery, combining correct methods with muscular co-ordination.

Social Aim: To teach economy, neatness and co-operation.

Ethical Aim: To give the student an appreciation of beauty, taste, and harmony to give a true conception of home life and its relation to the education of the girl.

General Statement

The importance of this department in the school will be stressed more this year than heretofore. The rooms and entire department will be newly equipped and so arranged that each young lady will be given individual attention. Some special lessons are best mastered in group work, or by direct demonstrations. In view of this fact, certain days are assigned for special lectures by the director with the student taking sufficient notes to enable them to make future reports upon the subject taught Individual work supplements lectures and group work.

COURSE OF STUDY

HOME ECONOMICS I.—*Cookery I.*—A study of the fundamental principles of cookery including the source, classification, food and economic values, preparation and preservation of the following foods: fruits, vegetables, cereals, eggs, milk and milk products, meat and fish. Two hours recitation and four hours laboratory per week.

HOME EC. V.—*Cookery II.* (cont.)—The principles in Cookery I applied to fats, salads, batters, doughs, ices and ice creams; also in planning of menus, marketing and introduction to preparation and serving of meals in the home. Two hours recitation and four hours laboratory per week.

HOME EC. II.—*Sewing I.*—A study of needlework and textiles including plain hand sewing, mending, embroidering, weaving, crocheting, tatting and knitting; a microscopic study of textile fibres, commercial weaves and physical tests of fibres and fabrics. One hour recitation and four hours laboratory per week.

HOME EC. VI.—*Millinery.*—This course includes the designing of patterns for hats, the use of wire and buckram in making shapes, use of straw, velvets and laces and the making of bows, flowers and other trimming. One hour recitation and two hours laboratory per week.

HOME EC. III.—*House Architecture and Sanitation.*—Historic and modern architectural styles and a study of problems involved in building a present day house including location, details of house construction, plumbing, heating, ventilation, lighting and sanitation. Discussion of efficient interior arrangements. Two hours recitation per week.

HOME EC. VII.—*Interior Decoration.*—A study of line and color in arangement of details in finishing and furnishing a room. The use of stencil, applique and dyeing in making designs for rugs, draperies, cushions, etc. A study of the period styles in furniture, rugs and pictures. One hour recitation and two hours laboratory.

HOME EC. IX.—*Cookery III.*—A course in which the chemical and physical properties of foods are studied with reference to the preparation and serving of typical meals in American homes, one meal to be prepared at each laboratory period. Two hours recitation and four hours laboratory per week.

HOME EC. XI.—*Nutrition and Dietetics.*—How to plan family dietary. Dietary standards, balanced rations and dietary needs as influenced by age, sex and occupation. Relation of nutrition to mental development. A study of invalid cookery and preparation of trays. Two hours recitation and four hours laboratory per week.

HOME EC. X.—*Elementary Dressmaking.*—This course covers the technique of machine sewing, the drafting of patterns and making of simple cotton garments and dresses with special reference to expenditure and wise choice of materials. Prerequisite: Sewing I. One hour recitation and four hours laboratory per week.

HOME EC. XII.—*Advanced Dressmaking.*—This course teaches the use of commercial patterns in making street, afternoon and evening costumes; a study of the history of costumes, of the ready-to-wear clothing industry; sweat shop labor; and laboratory practice in renovating and remodeling garments and dresses. One hour recitation and four hours laboratory per week.

HOME EC. VIII.—*Home Management.*—This course includes the planning of weekly duty schedules; working out of family budgets with regard to division of income; a study of the chemistry of cleaning as applied to fabrics, wood, metal, and crockery; and home care of the sick. One hour recitation and two hours laboratory per week.

HOME EC. IV.—*Bacteriology.*—A study of bacteria, yeasts and molds in the home. This includes conditions favoring growth, useful and harmful kinds of micro-organisms, preservation of foods and prevention of distribution of contagious diseases. One hour recitation and two hours laboratory per week.

XI.—PRACTICE TEACHING—Open to Seniors.

Textbooks

1 Kinnie & Cooley, Foods & Household Management.
2 Kinnie & Cooley, Foods & Household Management.
3 4 To be selected.

5 White's Successful Houses and How to Build Them.
6 Cooking Through the Preparation of Meals (School Home Economics at Chicago) also Rose's "Feeding the Family."
7 Standard Hospital Dietitians.
   McCollum & Davis, "Newer Knowledge of Nutrition," and others.
8 Book to be selected.
9 Library work.
10 Conn's "Bacteria, Yeast and Molds in the Home."

Department of Latin

PROFESSOR McALILEY

LATIN LABORATORY

Union University offers many advantages, and those in charge of the different departments are always alert to find those elements which will make for the interest and progress of the students.

Plans are being made for the installation of several hundred dollars' worth of new equipment for the Latin department for next y ear. This equipment will consist of a very fine high-powered stereopticon and a large number of sets of lantern slides which will show a great fund of interesting things concerning Roman life and culture, architecture, communication and travel and the like. These pictures have been gathered from the best specimens of the great artists and many of them have been made from the actual articles themselves. These pictures will be given to the Latin classes throughout the year in the form of illustrated lectures. This course itself will be worth coming a long way to get it.

Other features will be introduced into the class work of this department, all of which will make the class work of the different courses interesting and instructive.

If you are planninig to complete a college course and you expect to be a well-rounded, broadly-trained college man or woman, do not permit the vociferous arguments of the inexperienced to persuade you that you will have no need of a thorough working knowledge of Latin language and literature. You may have had some Latin and you may not care much for it, but bear in mind that you have not had it as it is given at Union University. COME AND SEE.

Observe that every italicized word below is derived from a Latin word.

Lux et veritas

Light and Truth

Prejudice is an *opinion* or *judgment formed* without due *examination.* It is *forming* a *verdict* before the *evidence* is in. This *preconceived decision* is, perhaps, the *maximum cause* why so much is *affirmed* about the *difficulty* and *impracticability* of *Latin.*

When rightly· *presented,* there is, perhaps no other *language* so simple in *syllabication* and *pronunciation.* One who knows can *demonstrate* the *fact* that the *percentage* of English words *derived* from *Latin* will be from thirty to sixty-five *percentage* on any page of English *diction.* This *fact confirms* two *important* facts in *additions primarily* that the *multitude* of *Latin derivatives* in the English makes it *possible* to *acquire* a·*Latin vocabulary* with *facility; sceondarily* this *fact demands conclusively* that, if one is *intending* to *consider* himself *educated* and *capable* of *comprehending* the root meanings of a *multitude* of English words, he must of *necessity* have a *potential* working knowledge of *Latin,*

You may have *decided* that you do not want *Latin.* That it is a *useless subject.* Maybe you have *studied* it a little and do not like it. But *remember* that you have not had the *opportunity* to *study Latin* as it is taught in *Union University.* Ask the *students* who have *completed* a *successful course* in the *language* and they will tell you that they not *only comprehend* the *subject,* but they had an *interesting* and pleasant time while doing so.

We have *courses* which will fit your case if you have never had any *Latin,* and if you are *prepared* for *college Latin,* a *veritable literary* feast awaits you in the *study* of *Cicero's* treatise on "Old Age" in the fall *term,* a *part* of *Livy's* history of the *Romans* in the winter *term and* a *number* of *selections* from *Horace's* poetry in the spring *term.* The work is *completed* in the Freshman *course,* and if you *desire* to *proceed* further in *Latin* history and biography and wish to *study* the *Roman* drama, the classes in the Sophomore *Latin* will meet your *demands splendidly.*

Any of these *courses* and others not *mentioned* may be *successfully* pursued and *completed* by *correspondence,* and the same *credit* will be given for the same amount of work done whether in class or by mail.

For the *convenience* of *students,* we give a *tabulated* list of *courses offered* with names of *texts, credits, etc.*

FOR FRESHMEN

LATIN I. *Translation* and sentence *structure study. Cicero's* De Senectute, Rockwood's *edition* with *vocabulary.* Fall *term,* three *recitations* a week. Three *hours credit.*

LATIN II. Livy's History, *selections translated* and parsing stressed. Burton's *text, Latin dictionary* and grammar needed. *Term* paper on a *subject* to be *assigned.* Winter *term,* three *recitations* a week. Three *hours' credit.*

LATIN III. *Study and interpretation* of *selections* from *Horace's* Odes. Moore's *text. Term* paper on *subject* to be *assigned.* Three *recitations* a week. Three *hours' credit.*

FOR SOPHOMORES

LATIN IV. A study of Latin biography and Latin drama. Gudeman's text of Agricola by Tacitus and Captivi by Plautus, Elmer's text. Term paper on some subject to be assigned. Fall term, two recitations a week. Two hours' credit.

LATIN V. A continued study of the Roman drama in a translation of Latin plays to be selected. Term paper on assigned subject. Winter term, two recitations a week. Two hours' credit.

LATIN VI. A thorough review of Latin principles in composition and a term paper in Latin of approximately 500 words on a subject to be assigned. Two recitations a week. Two hours' credit.

FOR TEACHERS

LATIN VII. This course is for those who have been teaching or are preparing to teach Latin. It consists of a thorough review of declensions, conjugations and other paradigms, Latin construction in parsing and composition. The subjects which are usually considered very difficult, such as Indirect Discourse, Sequence of Tenses, Purpose Clauses, Conditional Sentences, etc., are made clear and easy. Methods of pedagogical presentation will be given. Miss Sabin's Laboratory methods will be studied and practiced. The texts of the four high-school years of Latin will be reviewed. This course will be given if there is a sufficient demand for it. No special texts required. Three recitations a week throughout the year. Three hours' credit.

Department of Mathematics

DR. MALLORY

MATHEMATICS Ia, IIa, IIIa. *Unified Mathematics.*—Fall, Winter, and Spring terms. Meets Freshmen requirements. Intended especially for those that do not intend to take more than the minimum of mathematics.

Text: Karpinski, Benedict, and Calhoun's Unified Mathematics. Credit 12 hours.

MATHEMATICS I, II. *Trigonometry.*—Fall and winter terms. This course is required of Freshmen, not taking Unified Mathematics. Prerequisites: Entrance requirements in mathematics.

Text: Wentworth & Smith's Plane and Spherical Trigonometry. Credit 8 hours.

MATHEMATICS III. *Solid Geometry.*—Spring term. For those who take Trigonometry, the two meeting the Freshman requirements.

Text: Wentworth & Smith's Solid Geometry. Credit 4 hours.

MATHEMATICS IV, V, VI.—Throughout fall, winter and spring terms. The binominal theorem, convergency and divergeny of series, undetermined co-efficient, calculation of logarithms, permutations and combinations, probability, and elementarv theory of equations.

Text: Fite's College Algebra. Credit 9 hours.

MATHEMATICS VII, VIII.—Throughout fall and winter terms. Rectangular co-ordinates, the straight line, polar co-ordinates, transformation of co-ordinates, the circle, conic sections, tangents and normals. Elementary solid analytical geometry will be studied.

Text: Love's Analytical Geometry. Credit 6 hours.

MATHEMATICS IX.—Throughout spring term, five hours a week. In this course will be given the fundamental notions of Calculus. Practical applications will be made at each step to keep before the student the meaning and use of the symbols involved and to familiarize him with the underlying principles of the subject.

Text: Love's Differential and Integral Calculus. Credit 5 hours.

MATHEMATICS X.—*Surveying.*—This course is largely practical field work, and will embrace all the problems belonging to land surveying and the foundation principles of road construction and railroad lines, such as leveling, profiling, curves,

cross sections and mapping. The student will develop a prac-
tical familiarity with the transit; and plane tables, and other sur-
veying and engineering instruments.
Text: Wentworth & Smith. Credit 4 hours.
MATHEMATICS XI. *Analytical Mechanics.*—This course
is open only to those students who have completed Physics I and
Mathematics IX.
Text: Bowser's Analytical Mechanics. Credit 6 hours.
MATHEMATICS XII. A short course in differential equa-
tions will be offered alterating by years with Mathematics XI.
Prerequisites: Mathematics IX.
Text: Murray's Differential Equations. Credit 3 hours.

Department of Philosophy

DR. SAVAGE

(The J. R. Graves Chair of Logic and Moral Philosophy)

Logic

PHILOSOPHY I.—Although Logic is one of the oldest of the
sciences and in the hands of Aristotle nearly reached perfection,
yet in the last half century much has been added which will help
one in applying the tests of its rules.

On account of the difficulty in supplying a class with copies of
Davis' *Theory of Thought,* it has been decided to change to some
other text. Sellars will be used as a text in the discussion of the
nature of thought, and the many subdivisions of the science, on
which master minds have been working for more than 2,000
years.

The teacher will be under the necessity of supplementing the
text; and where such necessity exists, he will spare no pains in
supplying such teaching as he may deem important.

Mr. Sellars is one of the professors of philosophy in the University of Michigan, and the students may expect to have a man's
task. Six hours. Required of Juniors.

Ethics

It is highly important that college students be thoroughly
grounded in correct principles of Ethics before they encounter
the battles of life. Such training in the fundamental theories and
principles of morals and righteousness enables them to gauge

human conduct accurately and yet along broad lines, thus enabling them to make more correct analysis of human conduct and motives than would otherwise be possible. This will be valuable whether the student should practice Law, Medicine, enter the Ministry, be a Teacher, or simply be a student or actor in human relationships.

The development of the science of man in his group relations has given a new angle to Ethics. A new scientific study has been developed, known as Social Ethics. All of these phases of the subjects are taught in Union University. Six hours required of all Seniors.

Pre-Medical Course

For the benefit of those students who wish to prepare for entrance into any of the standard A-1 grade Medical Colleges, a two-years Pre-medical course is offered. The following course meets the requirements of standard medical schools, and those finishing it will be admitted without examination:

First Year		*Second Year*	
Chemistry 1 (4)	12	Chemistry 3 (5)	15
Mathematics 1 (4)	12	Physics 1 (3)	9
Biology 1 (3)	9	French or German (3)	9
French 1 or German (3)	9	Biology (3)	9
English 1 (4)	12	Elective (3)	9

The courses in Chemistry consist of three hours of recitation and six hours of laboratory work in Inorganic Chemistry. The courses in Biology consist of three hours recitation and three hours laboratory work. No student can enter the course in Physics I who has not taken Mathematics I. French or German must be continued through the second year. Elective courses in the following subjects are recommended by the Medical Council: Psychology, Economics, History, Sociology, Latin, and Greek.

REMARK.—All students who complete the Pre-medical Course and do one additional year of prescribed work in Union University may receive the A. B. degree upon completing one year in an approved Medical School. The work must be certified to Union University by the first of April preceding the commencement, and student must have been approved as a candidate by the faculty, upon application, by October 15, preceding. A satisfactory thesis upon an approved subject must be presented.

Science

PROF. PRINCE
PROF. DUNN
DR. DAVIS
DR. MALLORY

The courses in Science are offered for the purpose of general culture as well as to lay a proper foundation for those desiring to specialize in scientific work, in medicine, agriculture, or engineering. The keeping of note-book records is insisted upon.

The laboratory fee in each case covers all necessary material, but the student is required to pay for the breakage of all apparatus charged to him.

Lecture Room

This room is on the first floor of Barton Hall, and seats about fifty persons. The seats rise rapidly to the rear, thus enabling any one in the room to view any demonstration on the lecture desk in front, which is amply supplied with appliances and connections for water, gas and electricity. The windows are provided with blinds, thus enabling the room to be darkened for light experiments and for the use of a projection lantern, or moving pictures.

Laboratories.

The Chemical Laboratories for inorganic and qualitative chemistry are in a well lighted and commodious basement room. The laboratories for qualitative, organic and advanced work are immediately above on the first floor. These are equipped with water, gas, electricity, direct draught hoods, etc. The students' desks have been designed according to the most modern ideas, being provided with acid-proof alberene stone tops, sinks and troughs, reagent shelves in the middle over troughs and individual lockers, water and gas supply.

The physical and biological laboratories are in rooms adjoining the chemical laboratories and are similarly equipped. For advanced work in physics a basement room with solid concrete floor is used, thus avoiding all vibrations from the rest of the building. Special tables are provided and the apparatus is ample for giving numerous and standard experiments. A dark room located between the chemical and physical laboratories is convenient for work in light, spectroscopy, and photography.

For biological work there are supplied a number of compound dissecting microscopes, jars, trays, preserved specimens, etc.

An automatic still furnishes an ample supply of distilled water for all laboratory work.

Department of Biology

DR. DAVIS
PROF. STOVALL

BIOLOGY I.—General Biology. Fall term. Lectures and recitations twice a week. One two-hour laboratory period once a week.

This is an introductory course to all further work in biology and will give a general view of the structure and functions of animals; laboratory methods of dissection will be introduced; the student will be made familiar with the use of the compound microscope.

BIOLOGY II.—Invertebrate Zoology. Winter term. Lectures and laboratory hours as in Fall term. Prerequisite: Biology I.

This course consists of a comparative study of the various types of invertebrate life, their structure, development, relations and geographical distribution. The laboratory work will consist of dissection, microscopical examination and drawings of specimens studied.

BIOLOGY III.—Vertebrate Zoology. Spring term. Lectures and laboratory hours as in Fall term.

A study of the comparative morphology of a series of vertebrate forms will be made. Special emphasis given to the mammalia. Considerable attention will be given to embryology.

BIOLOGY IV.*—Botany. Fall term. Lectures and recitations twice a week. One two-hour laboratory period once a week.

A course consisting of the physiology and classification of plants. The important functions of plants will be demonstrated by numerous experiments.

BIOLOGY V.—Botany continued. Winter term. One recitation and two laboratory periods a week.

A general course covering algae, fugi, brophytes, pteridophytes and spermatophytes from the point of view of plant relationship, also embracing a study of their life, process of nutrition and reproduction.

BIOLOGY VI.—Bacteriology. Spring term. Three hours a week. One-half time given to laboratory work.

The work begins with the study of morphology of both pathogenic and non-pathogenic bacteria. In the study of the pathogenic organisms students will have access to the Physician's Clinical Laboratory of which Dr. Davis is director. This will be of special advantage to pre-medical students.

BIOLOGY VII. Heredity.

BIOLOGY X. Soil Biology.—A study of the biological factors relating to soil fertility, including qualitative and quantitative determinations of the biochemical activities of soil micro-organisms. The process of nitrogen fixation, transformation and assimilation, and similar studies of other essential elements are taken up in detail. The organisms concerned with each process are isolated and studied in pure culture. Senior for agricultural students; elective for others. Spring term. Three hours. Three-fourths of time given to laboratory work. Prerequisite: Biology. VI.

Department of Chemistry

PROF. PRINCE
AND ASSISTANTS

General Organic Chemsitry

CHEMISTRY I.—Fall term. Lectures and recitations. Three days a week. Laboratory, two double periods a week at times to be arranged. Prerequisite: Elementary Physics. This course includes the nomenclature, the broader quantitative relations of the Chemical Elements and a particular study of the non-metallic elements. Credits 4 hours.

CHEMISTRY II.—Winter term. Lectures, recitations and laboratory as in Chemistry I, which is a prerequisite. Special emphasis will be laid upon the laws of dissociation and ionization. The study of the non-metallic elements will be completed. Credits 4 hours.

CHEMISTRY III.—Spring term. Lectures, recitations and laboratory as in Chemistry I and II, of which this is a continuation and forms with them a complete course in general Chemistry. The metallic elements will be particularly treated from the standpoint of elementary qualitative analysis. Credit 4 hours.

CHEMISTRY I (a).—Fall term. Open only to students who have completed a thorough laboratory course in High School. Lectures, recitations and laboratory as in Chemistry I; but more rapid progress will be attempted. Credit 4 to 6 hours.
CHEMISTRY II (a).—Winter term. Continuation of Chemistry I (a). Credit 4 to 6 hours.

Qualitative Analysis

CHEMISTRY IV.—Spring and Fall term. Prerequisite: General Inorganic Chemistry. This course consists of the identification and separation of the metallic elements. The course is broadly analytical and lays the foundation for all future work in Analysis. Lectures, conferences and laboratory work same as hours. Credit 5 hours.

Quantitative Analysis

CHEMISTRY V.—Fall and Spring. Gravimetric Analysis. Lectures and conferences twice a week. Laboratory, 10 hours per week to be arranged. For Sophomores and Juniors. Prerequsite: General Inorganic Chemistry and Qualitative Analysis. Credit 5 hours.

CHEMISTRY VI.—Winter and Summer term. Volumetric Analysis. Lectures, conferences and laboratory work same as Chemistry V, of which this is a continuation. Credits 5 hours.

Organic Chemistry

CHEMISTRY VII.—Winter term. Lectures, three hours per week. Laboratory, 6 hours. For Sophomores or Juniors. Prerequisites: General Inorganic Chemistry, Qualitative Analysis, and preferably, Quantitative Analysis. This course consists of a study of the Aliphatic Series of the Carbon compounds and their synthesis in the Laboratory. Should be taken by all students intending to study medicine or agriculture. Credits 5 hours.

Household Chemistry

CHEMISTRY VIII.—Spring term. Continuation of Chemistry VII. Study of Aromatic Hydrocarbons and derivatives. Credits 5 hours.

CHEMISTRY IX.—Fall term. This is a course designed especially to meet the needs of students in Domestic Science, and for those special students who are unable to take the General Course in Chemistry. Prerequisite: One unit of entrance Science. Credit 4 hours.

Agricultural Chemistry

CHEMISTRY X.—Quantitative Analysis. This course is arranged to meet the needs of students in Agriculture. The work begins with the analysis of soils, fertilizers and agricultural products, and is extended to analysis of other substances. Prerequisite: Organic Chemistry and Qualitative Analysis. Any term. Credit 5 hours.

Advanced Quantitative Analysis

X CHEMISTRY XI.—Any term. Lectures, conferences and laboratory work at hours to be arranged. Prerequisite: Chemistry V and VI. Open only to Seniors. This course will include special methods of Quantitative Analysis, Proximate Food Analysis, Fire Assay, Water and Gas analysis, or Electrolytic Methods may be taken, according to the needs of the class. The course will be largely laboratory work with collateral reading. Credit 5 hours.

Physical Chemistry

X CHEMISTRY XII.—Any term. For Seniors. This course will consist of an elementary study of Physical chemistry. Prerequisite: College Physics, Freshman Mathematics, and three years of Chemistry. Credit 3 hours.

Geology

PROF. STOVALL

GEOLOGY I.—Structural Geology. Fall term, two lectures a week. Open only to Juniors and Seniors. Prerequisite: One year of Biology and one year of Chemistry.

GEOLOGY II.—Dynamical Geology. Winter term, two lectures a week. Will consist of a study of the external and internal geological agencies and of the resulting changes in the earth's surface. Prerequisite: Same as in Geology I, of which this is a continuation.

GEOLOGY III.—Historical Geology. Spring term, two lectures a week. This course will consider the different geological periods and fossil remains of plants and animals. Prerequisite: Geology I and II, of which this is a continuation and with them constitute a complete course in Geology.

Department of Physics and Astronomy

PROF. DUNN

GENERAL PHYSICS.—This course may be taken by those who had no Physics, or only a brief High School course. Three lectures and four laboratory hours per week. The lectures will be fully illustrative.

Text: Crew's *General Physics*.

Prerequisite: Trigonometry.

This course will continue throughout the year and will be sub-divided as follows:

PHYSICS I.—Fall term. Mechanics, Molecular Physics and Heat. Credit 4 hours.

PHYSICS II.—Winter term. Magnetism and Electricity. Credit 4 hours.

PHYSICS III.—Spring term. Sound and Light. Credit 4 hours.

PHYSICAL MEASUREMENTS.—This course should be taken by those who expect to specialize in technical lines. One hour recitation and six hours laboratory work per week. The course is sub-divided as follows:

PHYSICS IV.—Fall term. This course will be largely laboratory work in Mechanics and Heat. One hour recitation and 6 hours laboratory work per week.

Text: Millikan's *Mechanics, Molecular Physics and Heat*.

Prerequisite: Freshman Mathematics and Physics I. Credit 4 hours.

PHYSICS V.—Winter term. Magnetism and Electricity.

Text: Millikan and Mill's *Electricity, Sound and Light*.

Prerequisite: Freshman Mathematics, Physics I and Physics II. Credit 4 hours.

PHYSICS VI.—Spring term. Sound and Light. Text same as Physics V. Prerequisite: Freshman Mathematics and Physics I and III. Credit 4 hours.

ASTRONOMY I.—Fall term. Lectures and recitations three hours per week. This is a general course in descriptive astronomy, with just enough attention given to the mathematical side to acquaint the student with the methods of computation and to give him confidence in conclusions reached. Observation work with the telescope and transit is stressed.

Prerequisite: Freshman Mathematics.
Text: Jacoby's *Handbook of Astronomy*. Credit 3 hours.
The next course must be taken to receive this credit.

ASTRONOMY II.—Winter term. This is a continuation of
Astronomy I. Much library reference work is required, and students are taught the use of the tables of the American Ephemeris
and Nautical Almanacs. Credits 3 hours.

Department of Social Science

DR. WATTERS

DR. HOGAN

DR. MANTEY

SOCIOLOGY I. *Preliminary Study.*—An original course
provided from outlines furnished by Dr. Watters. This course
covers definitions, objects, purposes, history of the development
of science, and a superficial survey of the entire field of pracitcal
sociology. This course is intended to thoroughly acquaint the
student with the nature and importance of the new field he is
entering and to arouse his intense interest in it. Three hours.

SOC. II. This is a text book course, which will deal lightly
with the fundamental principles of social science. Three hours.

SOC. III. This course will consist of a series of local surveys,
and thesis on general social problems. Three hours.

SOC. IV. The history and development of sociology; its present tendency and probable future course. Three hours.

SOC. V. Extended surveys, text book reviews, extensive and
intensive library work, thesis on special social problems involving original research work. Open to Seniors. Nine hours.

SOC. VI. Modern social problems. A critical analysis of
causes and proposed remedies. Extensive library work and book
reviews. For Seniors. Three hours.

Department of Theology

DR. PENICK

(The Benjamin Perry Chair of Bible Theology.)

REMARKS

Our Theological Department does not offer a seminary course, nor does it propose to offer a substitute for such a course. On the contrary, it is hoped that the work given will whet the appetite of students for a full course in some òne of our great seminaries.

A glance over our course of study will reveal the fact that we offer a most practical elementary course of study intended to accomplish the following objects:

First. To give a careful survey of the Old and New Testament, teaching the students how to study the Bible, how to interpret it, and to arouse a greater interest in its study.

Second. To give the students a preliminary preparation in the great fundamental theological truths of the Bible as held and interpreted by Baptists.

Third. To offer such advantages as ministerial students need to advance themselves as rapidly as possible in their ministerial work while in college; to enable them to develop their ministerial gifts along with their mental training, and to inspire them with a desire for a more thorough theological training.

Fourth. To give such a practical course in elementary theological branches as is needed by the great mass of young preachers or those more advanced in years who, for various reasons, will never be able to pursue a course of study in a theological seminary.

COURSES OF STUDY

The English Bible

The Bible Course will be divided into two sections, namely, the Old Testament, and the New Testament. These courses are to be preceded by courses numbers I to VI, inclusive.

Old Testament Theology

BIBLE X.—The Pentateuch and the first six historical books will be covered this term. Special attention will be given to difficulties in the next, false interpretations, and heretical doctrines. Suggestions and explanations as to times, places and subject matter. . Two hours.

BIBLE XI.—The last six historical books and the five poetical books will be studied in the same manner as in the first term. The best helps will be used in the interpretation of these books, and special attention will be given to the spiritual and devotional elements in each book. Two hours.

BIBLE XII.—The five major and the twelve minor prophets will be studied with efforts to get the viewpoint of each prophet, and to confine the teachings on the fulfilment of each to the statements of inspiration, thus avoiding vain speculation as to times, places, peoples, and doctrines. Two hours.

BIBLE XIII.—The purpose is to study the religion of the Old Testament in definite periods of Hebrew history. Davidson's "Old Testament Theology" will be used in connection with the Bible to give a comprehensive view of the doctrines of the Old Testament. Two hours.

BIBLE XIV.—This is to be a study of the Old Testament prophecies, with special reference to its principles, history and the Messianic elements. Davidson's Old Testament Prophecies will be the text. Attention will also be given to some theories of critics. Orr's "Problem of the Old Testament" will be considered. Two hours.

BIBLE XV.—This study will be in the Book of Psalms. It will be both doctrinal and devotional. Text: Robert's "The Poetry and Religion of the Psalms." Review and examinations at the close of each term. Two hours each week.

New Testament Theology

BIBLE XVI.—The study of the Book as a whole, with introductory studies of the books. This term will be given to the study of the four Gospels and the Acts of the Apostles. Attention will be given to the harmony, but the burden of the work will be to see Jesus as each writer saw Him, the methods Christ used, and the doctrines He taught will be carefully noted. The organization and beginning of the church will be studied. Close attention will be given to times, places, peoples, methods, and doctrines. The Book of Acts will be studied carefully as to the historical background of the Epistles. Different texts will be studied in the light of the best authors. The growth, development, and characteristics of the church will be noted. Two hours.

BIBLE XVII.—The Epistles of Paul and the General Epistles of James, Peter and Jude will be studied with reference to doctrines, church ordinances, practices and church discipline. Best helps will be used on each of these books. Two hours.

BIBLE XVIII.—The Gospel of John, his three epistles and the Book of Revelation, will be studied to get the best possible view of the Eternal World, the believing, receiving faith that he taught, and to experience the assurance that brings fulness of joy, that we may render better service to the Master and be more helpful to others. Best helps will be used on Revelation so as to avoid false interpretations, that only the truth may be learned. Two hours.

BIBLE XIX.—This will be a comprehensive study of the teaching of Jesus with other writers of the New Testament.
Text: Sheldon's *"The Theology of the New Testament."* Other helps will be used. Two hours.

BIBLE XX.—A close study of the teachings of Paul on the doctrines of God, Man, Sin, Salvation, Sanctity of the Church, Man's domestic and civil relations and duties.
Text: Stephen's *"Pauline Theology."* Two hours.

BIBLE XXI.—Special studies in the teachings of John, his Gospel, Epistles, and Revelation. Text book, Stephen's *"Johannane Theology."* Two hours each week. Review and examinations at the end of each term.

Elementary, or Beginners' Courses in Theology

THEOLOGY I.—The regular Sunday School course. Two hours.

THEOLOGY II, III.—The Post-Graduate Sunday School course. Two hours each term.
These two courses will give a full year's preparatory work for the regular Theological work as outlined below, and be very helpful to all Sunday School teachers and students.

Courses in Systematic Theology

THEOLOGY IV, V, VI.—This course is to train students in the fundamental truths of the Christian religion. Text books, "The Christian Religion in Its Doctrinal Expression," by Dr. E. Y. Mullens. Frequent references will be made to Boyce, and Strong, and Walker's "Philosophy of the Plan of Salvation." Dr. Mullen's book will be so divided that it can be covered in three terms, with reviews and examinations at the close of each term. Two hours each term.

Courses in Evangelism

This course is given to help students the better to carry out the Commission of the Master.

EVANGELISM I.—The study of the methods used, doctrines taught, and results gained by Christ and the Apostles. Text book, the New Testament. "Normal Evangelism," by O. O. Green, will also be used to see that the individuals and churches are the Lord's agencies which He would have us work in carrying out His will. Two hours.

EVANGELISM II.—The texts this term will be Dr. Scarbrough's "With Christ After the Lost," "The Preacher and Prayer," by Bound, "The Soul Winner," by Spurgeon, and references to other authors. Two hours.

EVANGELISM III,—Will use same texts as in second term, supplemented by close studies of doctrines involved in Evangelistic work and our obligations to all lost sinners and mistaught Christmas. Reviews and examinations each term. The City of Jackson, and adjacent territory, offers opportunities for soul-winners on the streets, in homes, stores and shops. Two hours each week. Two hours.

Church History—One Year

CHURCH HISTORY I.—This course is intended to present a clear outline of the political and religious world into which Christ was born and Christianity established; the constitution of churches; forms of opposition and methods of defenses; the rise of heretical bodies. Two hours each week.

CHURCH HISTORY II.—Christianity in the Medieval period; the rise of Mohammedanism; beginning of Catholicism; division between the East and the West; spread through the West to the Reformation. Two hours.

CHURCH HISTORY III.—The Reformation, its causes and results. Rise of the various denominations; the continuity of true churches through all ages. Two hours each week. Reviews and examinations each term.

Homiletics and Pastoral Theology

HOMILETICS I.—The Fall term will be devoted to a study of the sermon. Lectures will be given on the structure, style, and preparation of the sermon, and the methods of classifying sermons by methods of treatment, subjects, aim, process and history, and method of delivery. Sermon outlines furnished by the class are criticised, and there will be class quizzes and written examination. Elective. Two hours per week.

HOMILETICS II.—Winter term. The first half of this term will be devoted to Pastoral Theology. The relations and conduct of the pastor in his home, in the church, and in his social relations will be considered.

The second half of the term will be devoted to the study of typical sermons of men who have attracted attention as preachres. Such varied types of men as Spurgeon, Jos. Parker, Robert South, Alex. MacLaren, John Caird, Francis Wyland, Henry Ward Beecher, J. M. Pendelton, John A. Broadus, T. DeWitt Talmage, D. I. Moody, Phillips Brooks, J. B. Hawthorne, J. C. Hiden, A. C. Dixon, "Billy" Sunday, and Sam P. Jones will be studied with a view to learning what has given importance to the sermons published.

Elective. Two hours per week.

HOMILETICS III.—Spring term. A continuation of II, until the latter part of the term, when sermons will be required of members of the class for criticism by the class and professor.

Elective. Two hours per week.

Department of Music

MRS. A. W. PRINCE,
Director
Piano, Pipe Organ and Theory
Band and Orchestra Instruments

MR. WM. JAMES WORK,
Teacher of Voice Art of Singing

Introductory Statement

One great advantage of musical work in a college conservatory is the atmosphere of study and the literary opportunities that offer themselves.

It is advisable that music students carry some branches of the college course; and it is equally advisable that college students, if they have any musical talent, pursue some branch of musical work. Music is the art that appeals to the largest number of people. All boarding students must carry as much as fourteen hours work including their fine arts courses, unless upon advice of physician.

Curriculum

Pianoforte, Organ, Harmony, Theory, Musical History, Voice, Violin.

Pianoforte

The pianoforte occupies a place of dignity and value, and should have treatment commensurate with its place as a factor in musical education. The foundation of pianoforte technique is flexibility of the fingers, hand and arm. Next comes the acquirement of strength in these members. Then, building on this foundation, we form a correct musical touch.

The touch of the pianoforte, as well as other musical work, will be along really musical lines, the selection of exercise, study and piece being made with reference to their musical value, as well as to the special necessities of the pupil and the maintaining of a lively interest in her work. While the old classics will live on, much pedagogical music has gone out of date, and should be replaced by that which more truly represents the modern spirit and progress.

The curriculum is chosen from the standard composers, not omitting modern European and American writers. It is unnecessary to state the list in detail.

Harmony

Harmony, dealing with chord formation and progression, is a vital part of musical knowledge, and is necessary for the understanding of what one plays or hears. It bears the relation to music that grammar does to language, and hence is an essential part of a musician's equipment.

We aim to teach harmony in an interesting as well as thorough manner. The time required to complete the Harmony course is two years.

Text: Emory or Orene; Foote and Spaulding.

Outline of Piano Study

By the end of the first year, pupils should be playing music of the grade of Clementi's Sonatinas; second year, Czerny Kuhlau's and the easier Mozart Sonatas, and the easier Mendelssohn's Songs Without Words; third year, Cramer-Buloy studies, Clementi's Gradus, Bach's two-part and three-part Inventions, Beethoven's easier Sonatas, Chopin's easier works, Kullak's Octave Studies.

For the completion of full course, another year is required, including the Moscheles, Kessler, Henselt and Chopin Studies, as well as some of the Bach Fugues, Chopin's larger works, such as Op. 40, 29 and 31, and Beethoven's Sonatas, such as Op. 10, 13, 26 and 27.

The compositions here named represent only in a general way the stages of advancement. Such works are, of course, accompanied by the necessary technical studies and selections in free forms. To complete the full piano course with its adjunct theoretical studies takes pupils of fair talent not less than four years. Credit will be given for all previous study that has been done in a satisfactory manner. Especial attention is given to having the pupils acquire a practical reportoire of pieces for home and concert use.

The Pipe Organ

The course of study is based on the works of Stainer, Rinck, Buck, Thayer and selections from classics and modern organ composers.

It includes the necessary instruction in manual, pedal and registration to fit students for the position of church and concert organist.

Previous to studying organ, pupils must have had sufficient preparatory study on the piano. Technical knowledge and ability to read music readily at sight are necessary requirements for satisfactory organ study.

Musical History and Theory

The two branches are combined in one study.

Theory Outline: Acoustics, notation, musical terms and forms of composition; musical instruments; the orchestra.

History Outline: The rise and development of modern music; early church music; the opera; oratorio; instrumental music; the great composers, their works and characteristics; classic and romantic music; and understanding of all technical terms, with correct pronunciation of foreign terms and proper names. The time required to complete this course is two years.

Text: Hamilton's *Outline of Musical History,* and Baltzell's *History of Music.*

Keyboard Harmony and Memorizing

1—*Keyboard Harmony*

Keyboard Harmony consists in study at the keyboard of the primary chords and their connections, as they are used in musical compositions.

This study leads to improvisiations, and is the foundation of memorizing.

In the regular Harmony Course the work consists almost wholly of writing the chords and various harmonic progressions, pupils rarely obtaining more than a theoretical knowledge of the subject.

The practical work in keyboard harmony is plainly necessary for all students of piano or organ. It may precede or follow the regular Harmony Course.

Text: Homann's *Harmony Primer*.

2—Memorizing

The prevalent custom of pianists to play without the music, giving entire programs in this manner, makes it necessary that the ability to memorize be required. The mechanical process of memorizing by note—that is, playing the notes and repeating them—is decidedly unreliable, the pupil wasting time and energy, while the result is nearly always one of uncertainty. The understanding of several distinct agencies is necessary for satisfactory memorizing. They are:

1. Familiarity with the elementary material of music—scales and chords, measures and rythm.

2. The principles of harmonic progression.

3. Analysis of musical design.

4. Conventional outlines of form which tend to reveal the order of tonality of different divisions and subdivisions in certain styles of music.

The time required to complete the course in the two studies, taking one-half hour private lessons a week, will be about one year.

Text: *Guide to Memorizing,* Goodrich.

Students on campus are not permitted to take studies with outside persons without special permission from faculty.

Voice Culture

WM. JAMES WORK,
Director and Instructor

Voice Culture and Chorus

Singing is probably the most difficult of all specialties of music, since it is apparently the easiest thing of all things musically to do; for, when there is aresonate larynx and a good ear, one can, by a certain happy instinct, accomplish something that touches the heart of the untutored; it is usually taken for granted that nothing is easier than to sing. The precise reverse is the actual fact. Few studies require a keener mind, more patience and more artistic environment than the human voice.

Cultivation of the voice in singing is now regarded as an important branch of education. Like many natural powers, the voice is given to us in crude state and we are obliged to develop it through means that art has revealed to us.

Students enter grades at the judgment of the director, and the course largely depends upon the individual needs of each. It has for its object a high degree of perfection in church, oratorio and concert singing, familiarity with the vocal schools and works of great masters, and those principles of vocal culture so necessary for successful teaching. A general outline of the course is given but adapted to the needs of individuals.

Students will be graded on same basis as in literary work.

Preparatory Course.

All candidates for entrance to the Freshman year of the regular diploma vocal course, will be required to meet some conditions in voice and literary work as candidates in Pianoforte Department.

Preparatory vocal work consists of elementary voice training, principles of breathing, voice placing and development of tone and elementary vocalizes, according to individual requirements.

Sight Singing, Ear Training and Musical Appreciation.

The Regulation Diploma Course

Grade I.

English, French or one other foreign language; Sight Singing; Ear Training; two voice lessons a week; one practice period daily.

Continuation of Voice Training, Vocal Technique, Art of Vocalization, Vocalizes Studies and Songs selected in reference to particular points in vocal development and enunciation.

Appearance on private matinee programs.

Elective. Extra hours required.

Grade II.

English, French or some other foreign language; Sight Singing, Harmony, Chorus. Two Voice lessons per week, two-third grade Piano lessons per week, one practice period daily.

Voice Training, Advanced Vocalization; Songs, Classic and Modern English, and Oratorio. Singing in public recitals.

Elective. Extra hours required.

Grade III.

Philosophy, Advanced Sight-singing, Vocal Ensemble Music, Harmony, History of Music, Chorus.

Two lessons per week, one practice period daily.

Voice Production—Art of Vocalization and Musical Embelishments. Italian, French and English Songs. Advanced study or Oratorio and church music, Folk Songs. Chorus work. Frequent appearance in public recitals.

Elective. Extra hours required.

Grade IV.

Philosophy, two Voice lessons per week, one practice period. Special attention given to appreciation of music and the building of a repertoire.

Requirements for Concert Diplomas

Candidates for Diplomas will be required to have two years of Harmony, two years of History of Music, two years of Solfeggio and in addition one year of advanced Sight-reading of ensemble music. The first three grades of the Pianoforte Course, or their equivalent, covering Freshman and Sopohomore years. One year of French, Spanish or German with Italian Diction, together with the required number of literary studies indicated in each year of the respective courses will be required.

Frequent and successful public appearances, together with a creditable final Graduation Recital, are included.

The Teacher's Diploma and Certificate

This diploma is issued upon the same conditions as the Concert Diploma, excepting the final Graduating Recital. Candidates must also have done some practical teaching or coaching under the supervision of the teacher. Certificates can be issued to those not able to take the full diploma, but this implies a fair amount of the regular course and merely certifies as to the work covered.

Glee Club for Men and Women

The members of the club are chosen from the more advanced voice pupils and any others who have good voices. It is the aim of the Director to make the organization worthy of membership and an honor for the individual to belong to it.

Gospel Music

A course in the study of Gospel Hymns is of great benefit to young people who intend to do any kind of Christian work.

To know how to sing and to interpret a hymn is a great help in a religious service. The pastor or teacher who can lead the people in a song will find that he has opened the way for the message which is to follow.

A course in the study of hymns and hymn singing is offered once a week.

Band and Orchestra Department

RAYMOND GUYON, Director
Concert Violinist, Conductor, Theorist

French extraction, born in Denver, Colorado; attended Denver Public Schools, and one year Denver University. First music lesson taken at an early age. Studied 'cello and brass instruments under Latton and Reisner. Later studied violin. Employed as professional musician and teacher until 1914, at which time removed to Texas, going to Marfa, Texas, to take charge of Marfa Symphoney Orchestra and Marfa Brass Band. In 1916 removed to Silver City, New Mexico, where employed as first violin in Silver City Symphony Orchestra, and as teacher. Removed to El Paso in 1917, where employed as first trombone in municipal band, and in summer of 1917 directed feature orchestra at Cloudcroft, New Mexico, largest summer resort in Southwest. From fall of 1917 until 1920 directed orchestra at the Raleigh Hotel, Waco, Texas, during which time studied as graduate student under Anton Navaratil, at Baylor University, who is pupil of Sevrik, probably the greatest violin teacher in the world today. In fall of 1920 took charge of band and orchestra department at Rusk College, Rusk, Texas; in 1922 made dean of entire Conservatory of Fine Arts Department.

* * * *

MRS GWENDOLYN STEVENSON GUYON, Director
Clarinetist, Cornetist, Saxophonist, Conductor, Composer

Born in Davenport, Iowa, attended public and high schools at Davenport; First music lessons at early age under her father who was well-known bandmaster in Iowa. Member of many professional ladies' bands and orchestras. Much professional and teaching experience in Chicago, Davenport and other cities. Studied under many well-known musicians; many successful pupils. Soloist with ladies' orchestra at World's Fair at San Francisco in 1915; director Elks' Band, Silver City, New Mexico; joint experience with Raymond Guyon, Cloudcroft, New Mexico, El Paso, Texas, Waco, Texas, (Director of Orchestra Auditorium in Waco), Assistant Director Band and Orchestra Department Rusk College, Rusk, Texas, 1920-23.

* * * *

PURPOSE

It is the aim of this department to provide a cultural subject for each student which will be of practical use and benefit all through life.

The study of some band and orchestral instrument will not only provide the student with the means of gratifying his desire to play good music whenever he wants to, but will give him a practical profession which may, at his option, be turned into a source of income. Aside from these benefits, the student will derive pleasure all through the years of life from his association with other musical people in the bands and orchestras which have been formed all over the country in late years, he will be an asset to the social and intellectual life of his community through his ability to give pleasure to others, and will be able to enrich the church service by means of his talent.

SCOPE

All instruments used in the modern bands and orchestras are correctly taught in this department, while practical experience is provided the student through the activities of the student band and orchestra maintained by this department. Such special theoretical subjects as harmony, counterpoint, instrumentation, etc., will be offered as required.

GENERAL INFORMATION

The instruments of the modern concert band are roughly divided into three classes: brasses, wood-winds and percussion instruments. The brass instruments are (1) the Saxhorn family, which contains the cornet, alto, baritone and bass or tuba, (2) the French horn, (3) the trombone. The wood-winds comprise (1) the flute and piccolo, (2) the clarinet, alto clarinet and bass clarinet, and (3) the oboe and bassoon. The percussion instruments are those which, as the name implies, are made to sound through being struck, as, for instance, bass and snare drums, tympani or kettle drums, bells, chimes, etc.

The instrumentation of the modern symphony orchestra is divided into four classes: strings, brasses, wood-winds and percussions. The string instruments are (1) the violin family, consisting of the violin, viola, violin-cello and double or contra-bass, and (2) the harp. The wood-winds used are flute, oboe, clarinet and bassoos. Of the brass family, only the trumpet, trombone, French horn and tuba are used, the instruments of the Saxhorn family being of such a nature that their tone will not penetrate through the mass of strings.

The Saxophone family, consisting of soprano, alto, tenor, baritone and bass, is neither a brass nor a wood-wind, but partakes of the nature of each, in that it is made of brass but is played with a reed and wooden mouth-piece. It combines the mellow quality of the brass with the penetrating quality of the wood-wind, and has become very popular within the last few years—

in fact, there are more people studying saxophone in America today than any other instrument excepting the piano. It is used in
both band and orchestra, but in orchestra it is used principally as
a substitute for some other instrument, there being no regular arrangement made in orchestral instrumentation for its use. We
offer an especially strong course for the saxophone. Many music teachers offer to teach the saxophone in three months. We
do not make any guarantee as to the length of time required to
learn this instrument, but we have known of cases where the student learned to play church songs in one week's time.

Department of Elocution and Oratory

The purpose of the study of reading and speaking is to develop one's powers along two lines—Interpretation and Expression. One may grasp thought but not be able to express it to
others with the force and clearness to make it effective. Drill
along the line prescribed in this department develops power to
both interpret and reproduce. This is best developed by practice
in reading and speaking. To interpret readily one must have
ready insight into the structure of language. Practice alone can
develop along such lines. The proper study of expressions develops one along these lines as nothing else ever can.

Development of memory and the imagination is one of the
greatest benefits derived from this study. Without memory a
man is always at a disadvantage; without imagination he is a
dullard and incapable of refinement. Testimony to increasing
ease in learning lessons in other studies and an enlarged appreciation in many lines of thought and observation is constant on
the part of those who have attained appreciable proficiency.

The course of study is intended to be adapted to the needs of
individual pupils. Special attention will be given to the construction of masterpieces; also to analysis of subjects, impromptu
debates, sermon building, etc. The psychological basis of expression is constantly sought for. The Emerson, Del Sarte
Physical Culture will be given free.

Four years of college work is required for the Bachelor's Degree in this department. By four years of college work we mean
that the student must meet college entrance requirements, and do
192 hours of college work, including the four yars of expression.
Certificates given on completion of course with less than the col-

lege requirement in other studies. One year of college English in addition to a high school course is required for certificate

COURSE OF STUDY

First Year

1. Enunciation and Articulation.
2. Modulation as to Pitch.
3. Tuning the Ear.
4. Cultivation of Memory, Dixon Method.
5. Interpretation and Reading.

Second Year.

1. Psychology of Expression. Curry.
2. Method of Effective Speaking. Phillips.
3. Study of Tone Color.
4. Touch, Rate, Force, Proportion.

Third Year.

1. Cultivation of the Imagination. Curry.
2. Laws of Expression. Fenno.
3. Scripture and Hymn Reading.
4. Stimulation of Animation.

Fourth Year.

1. Cultivation of the Historic Instinct. Curry.
2. Study of Shakespeare and other Masters.
3. Analysis, Speech-formation, or Sermon Building. (For preachers.)
4. Book-cutting, Arranging Programs, Stage Management.
5. Impromptu Debating.

In all the courses constant practice in recitation of memorized selections will be required. Lectures as deemed advisable will be given.

Del Sarte Physical Culture free.

NOTE.—The new head of this department will doubtless change materially the above course of study.

Union University Training School

FACULTY

N. M. STIGLER, A. M.,
(Union University)
English

MRS. L. D. RUTLEDGE, A. M.,
(George Peabody)
French and Mathematics

W. L. HOUSE, A. B.,
(Union University)
Bible and History

MISS GRACE POWERS, A. B.,
(Graduate Home Economics)
(Union University)
Home Economics

(To be supplied.)
History

MRS. A. J. ROBINSON, A. B.
(University of Texas)
Assistant in English

MISS VERA ROUTON
Spanish

(To be supplied)
Latin

(To be supplied)
Mathematics

(To be supplied)
Latin and Spanish

This school is standard, being on the accredited list and a member of the Southern Association of Schools and Colleges, and graduates from it are accepted without examination in all of the leading colleges and universities in the United States, including West Point Academy and Annapolis.

REMARK.—By order of the Board of Trustees, the Training School will be discontinued after June 1, 1924. However, we will still make provision to care for students above 20 years of age who may lack a little of having finished all of their high school education. Details will be explained upon request.

COURSE OF STUDY

This is standard four-year high school, offering all of the regular high school work. Any one interested should write for special bulletin giving further information.

ADVANTAGES

The following are among the special advantages offered in the training school:

1. A full four-year course, so organized that the student is promoted by subject rather than classes, so that the students are not promoted or demoted by grades, but are allowed to advance in all subjects in which he makes good, and is retarded only in those in which he fails.

2. A strong faculty.

3. Fine Christian influence.

4. The inspiring atmosphere of the college and college student body with which they associate in chapel exercises, athletics and other functions.

5. Excellent equipment.

6. Character of work which we guarantee to be far above that usually given.

7. Thoroughly standard, diplomas received at par everywhere.

8. Splendid discipline, that restricts without crushing, directs and inspires.

9. Mature boarding students only solicited. Young students who require constant watching or military discipline should not be sent to our school.

10. Rates reasonable, for one-half and less than one-half the cost in most great training schools of the land where anything like equal advantages are given.

Anyone interested should write for special Training School Bulletin.

Address   N. M. STIGLER, Principal,

Jackson, Tenn.

Jackson School of Business

CHAS. A. DERRYBERRY, M. Accts., Principal .
Advertising, Office Practice, and Employment

ROMUS MASSEY
Bookkeeping and Accounting

MRS. JIMMIE DEMENT ANDERSON
(Graduate Gregg School)
Principal of Shorthand Department
Shorthand, Civil Service, Court Reporting

MISS JOHNNIE MAI GUTHRIE
Principal Typewriting Department
Touch Typewriting, Speed Classes

The School of Business has entered on its thirty-sixth year of continuous, successful operation. The school has been under the present management for nineteen years. Th plans for the work this year include a more extensive and comprehensive training for its students than we have ever given before. We will be in position, both in point of teaching force and in equipment, to do more work and get better results for the student than we have at any time in the past.

The School of Business was admitted to membership in the National Association of Accredited Commercial Schools almost two years ago. This means that our courses, our teachers, our equipment, and other things that go to make up a first-class Business School, have been passed upon by the highest authority in Commercial Education. An Accredited Business College bearts the same relation to first-class business enterprises that an Accredited High School bears to a Standard College. Before selecting a commercial school, you should be sure that the school is fully accredited.

The School of Business will hereafter be housed in the new building to be erected for the University Training School. Its close proximity to Union University and the contact the business students will have with more than a dozen great educators, affords a tremendous power in the development of personality in the individual student. The associations and environments in every way are of the best. A student taking a business course under such advantages has an opportunity to succeed at least two or three times better than a student who is trained separate and apart from such opportunities. One can not realize the tremendous force of these advantages until he has come in actual touch with them.

We maintain a thoroughly efficient teaching force all the time. Our faculty for this year is made up of men and women who are graduates of the very best business colleges and business training schools that the country affords. They are men and women of experience, both in teaching and in practicing the things that they teach. A prospective student can rest assured of the fact that this school will never maintain anything but a first-class teaching force. When it becomes necessary to make a change for any reason, it is always our aim to improve our teaching force with every change. The present teaching force is large enough to give all the individual instruction that is necessary for the rapid advancement of the individual student. Our class work is enthusiastic and extremely helpful. No better class work can be found anywhere.

It has been the aim of the present management of the School of Business to maintain a business college of the very highest type of efficiency. It has been the aim to solicit that class and type of young men and young women of the very highest order. In training such students, we recognize the fact that we are in position to serve the very best business firms. It is with this class of business that a young man or a young woman has an opportunity to succeed. It has also been our aim to maintain an institution of this high order at the lowest possible expense to the individual student. You will, therefore, find that our tuition rates on all courses fall far below the corresponding rates of other similar institutions. We also maintain an extensive and thoroughly efficient Employment Department, which is operated free of cost to the individual student.

We hope you will be kind enough to write us for information regarding our courses; the rates of tuition, expense, and for any other information that you may desire. Address all correspondence to C. A. Derryberry, Principal, Post Office Box 333, Jackson, Tennessee.

REMARK I.—The Jackson School of Business is the personal property of Mr. C. A. Derryberry, and is connected with the University Training School for the mutual benefit of both. The business management is entirely separate, neither having any connection with nor responsibility for the other.

REMARK II.—On or before June 1, 1924, Mr. Derryberry will remove his School of Business from the University to a down-town location and will have no further connection with the college.

Addenda

Since the preceding pages have gone to press, we find it necessary to add the following information:

ADDITIONAL INFORMATION CONCERNING HOME ECONOMIC COURSES.

I. ELEMENTARY DESIGN.—A study of the arrangement of lines, forms, balance and rhythm; design in black and white, color. One hour lecture, four hours laboratory. Three hours' credit per term.

II. COSTUME DESIGN.—The study of line, form and color as applied to dress.

III. INTERIOR DECORATION.—The study of color and design and arrangement of furniture in the home. One hour lecture, two hours laboratory. Two hours credit per term.

Further instruction in drawing, water color and oil painting will be given if requested. Art 1, 2, 3 are required of all Home Economic students.

PHYSIOLOGY, HYGIENE AND SANITATION.

Fall, Winter, Spring, 6 Hours.

This course is designed to meet the needs of students who are specializing in Home Economics and is an elementary study of the structure and functions of the human body, the principles governing its proper care, and the cause, course and prevention of the most common diseases, with emphasis on general health.

CERTIFICATE COURSE.

Home Economics I, II, III	9 Hours
(Cookery)	
Home Economics IV, V, VI	9 Hours
(Clothing)	
Chemistry I, II, III	9 Hours
English	9 Hours
Education	9 Hours
	45 Hours

DIPLOMA COURSE

Subjects offered in Certificate Course plus—

Nutrition and Dietetics	3 Hours
Home Nursing	3 Hours

Home Management ....3 Hours
Design ....2 Hours
Architecture ....2 Hours
Interior Decorating ....2 Hours
Millinery ....2 Hours
Household Physics ....3 Hours
Household Chemistry ....3 Hours
Biology ....3 Hours
Bacteriology ....3 Hours
Physiology ....3 Hours
Organization ....1 Hour
Practice Teaching ....2 Hours
Education ....9 Hours

DEGREE COURSE.

Those desiring the degree of Bachelor of Science in Home
Economics must meet college entrance requirements and will, in
addition to the studies required for the Diploma Course, do
enough of the regular required work in the college to make 192
hours.

COURSE LEADING TO THE BACHELOR OF MUSIC DEGREE.

First Year

Credit

Advanced Piano or Voice or Violin (2 hours daily
    practice) ....12 Hours
Harmony ....3 Hours
English (Freshman) ....12 Hours
Foreign Language (Modern)...9 Hours
Music Minor ....6 Hours
Literary Electives ....6 Hours

48 Hours

Second Year

Advanced Harmony ....3 Hours
History of Music ....3 Hours
Advanced Piano, Voice or Violin (2 hours daily
    practice) ....12 Hours
Foreign Language ....9 Hours
*Physics of Sound (Physics III) ....4 Hours
Music Minor ....5 Hours
Literary Electives ....12 Hours

48 Hours

Third Year

Advanced Piano, Voice or Violin (3 hours daily
    practice) ....15 Hours
Minor in Music .... 6 Hours
Educational Psychology and Methods .... 9 Hours
English (Sophomore) .... 6 Hours
History (Musical) .... 3 Hours
Recitals .... 3 Hours
Literary Electives .... 6 Hours

                                   48 Hours

Fourth Year

Advanced Piano, Voice or Violin (5 hours daily
    practice) ....15 Hours
Minor Subject .... 6 Hours
Practice Teaching .... 3 Hours
Recitals .... 3 Hours
Education .... 9 Hours
Literary Electives ....12 Hours

                                   48 Hours

*If not taken in High School.

Degrees Conferred

May 30th, and at close of Summer School August 11, 1923.

Bachelor of Arts

Acklin, Robert, Memphis, Tenn.
Bickers, Horace Anderson, Ripley, Tenn.
Bodkin, Luther, Wyckliffe, Ky.
Brown, J. O., Lexington, Tenn.
Carter, Mary, Bolivar, Tenn.
Collins, J. Floyd, Ozark, Ala. (As of year 1876).
Dance, James Claude, Mayfield, Ky.
Dexter, Miriam Estelle, Baptist Hospital, Memphis, Tenn.
Dorris, Jewell Mays, Bolivar, Tenn.
Easley, Howard, Martin, Tenn.
Etheridge, Lelia Fay, Jackson, Tenn.
Franks, Susie Jones, Jackson, Tenn.
Fulmer, Maurice Meredith, Idabel, Okla.
Gilliam, Norris, Bells, Tenn.
Gilbert, Loreen, Jackson, Tenn.
Gooch, Lena, Selmer, Tenn.
Horn, Ivan Newton, Westport, Tenn.
Huckaba, Carey Judson, Huntingdon, Tenn.
Hargrove, B. L., Farmington, Ky.
Hall, B. F., Dyer, Tenn.
Jackson, Virginia, Jackson, Tenn.
Jones, Mrs. Linnie Elizabeth, Jackson, Tenn.
Johnson, Horace Whitfield, Jackson, Tenn.
Jamerson, L. W., Collierville, Tenn.
Koffman, Irby, Humboldt, Tenn.
Louis, Howard E., Jackson, Tenn.
McKendree, Eva F., Arlington, Ky.
McKnight, Mary, Malesus, Tenn.
McMillan, Mrs. J. O., Collierville, Tenn.
Muller, Damaris Jaccard, Montbiliard, France.
Pettigrew, Willie R., Jackson, Tenn.
Polk, Clyde Festus, Slidell, La.
Powers, Grace Alberta, Selmer, Tenn.
Patrick, Frances, Memphis, Tenn.
Pennington, J. A., Mercer, Tenn.
Pinkston, C. B., Adamsville, Tenn.
Smith, Xena Lou, Amory, Miss.
Smith, Robert N., Jackson, Tenn.
Stallings, Edith, Halls, Tenn.
Strong, Annie, Cordova, Tenn.
Smith, J. Simon, Bolivar, Tenn.
Stephenson, G. D., Finley, Tenn.
Todd, Alvin, Dickson, Tenn.
Witherington, A. M., Sharon, Tenn.
Waldrop, Homer H., Idlewild, Tenn.

Bachelor of Science

Brasher, Phelan, Jackson, Tenn.
Castellaw, Roland K., Maury City, Tenn.
Cole, Cecil H., Milan, Tenn.
Davis, C. E., Montezuma, Tenn.
Hodge, James L., McKenzie, Tenn.
Jones, N. R., Memphis, Tenn.
Lewis, Talmadge K., Jackson, Tenn.

Malone, George K., Jackson, Tenn.
Pope, W. W., Jackson, Tenn.
Roberts, Allison Hardee, Key West, Fla.
Roland, C. P., Pocahontas, Tenn.
Rutledge, Ray W., Jackson, Tenn.
Taylor, Asa M., Rutherford, Tenn.
Wilson, W. E., Martin, Tenn.

Normal Diploma

Brasher, Phelan, Jackson, Tenn.
Curlin, Ida, Brownsville, Tenn.
Hundley, Neil, Mercer, Tenn.
Kirkman, Bruce E., Union City, Tenn.
McMinn, Gladys, Trenton, Tenn.
Mewborn, Mary K., Macon, Tenn.
Pennington, Sara Helen, Mercer, Tenn.
Spann, Liza, Murray, Ky.
Pinkerton, Lucille, Centerville, Tenn.

Graduates in Home Economics
Diplomas

Carter, Marye, Bolivar, Tenn.
McKendree, Eva Ford, Arlington, Ky.
Pinkerton, Lucille, Centerville, Tenn.
Rose, Mrs. Mamie, Grand Junction, Tenn.
Smith, Xena Lou, Amory, Miss.

Certificates

Gilbert, Claire, Paris, Tenn.
Gilbert, Loreen, Jackson, Tenn.
Kirkman, Bruce E., Union City, Tenn.

Bachelor of Music

Harris, Pearl Elizabeth, Stanton, Tenn.
Ballard, Mary Salome, Memphis, Tenn.

Post-Graduate in Music

Watters, Lillian, Jackson, Tenn.

Diploma in Music

Nance, Lila Ray, Ripley, Miss.
Jernigan, Annie, Jackson, Tenn.
James, Mary, Humboldt, Tenn.
Heaslet, Inez, Clinton, Ky.

Graduates of University Training School

Barrix, Stokey A., Humboldt, Tenn.
Benge, Louise, Humboldt, Tenn.
Boothe, Lela Mai, Jones, Tenn.
Collins, Clara Beatrice, Halls, Tenn.
Campbell, Clyde R., Jackson, Tenn.
Carlson, C. C., Jackson, Tenn.
Cole, Ira C., Trenton, Tenn.
Deaton, Willie, Bethel Springs, Tenn.
Duke, Ola, Jackson, Tenn.
Fitzgerald, C. W., Jackson, Tenn.
Gwaltney, Ernest, Dyersburg, Tenn.
Halford, Rachel, Jackson, Tenn.
Howard, M. B., Paducah, Ky.
Herbert, Agnes, Galt, Mo.
Moore, John Frank, Halls, Tenn.

Moore, Russell Lee, Halls, Tenn.
Morrison, R. E., Jackson, Tenn.
Morrison, Mrs. R. E., Jackson, Tenn.
Patterson, Russell B., Trenton, Tenn.
Rice, Marion, Jackson, Tenn.
Robbs, Hilda Mai, Jackson, Tenn.
South, Alta, Poden, Miss.
Taylor, Allene, Greenfield, Tenn.
Williams, Maness, Selmer, Tenn.
Williams, Waldemar, Bethel Springs, Tenn.
Williams, Mildred, Jackson, Tenn.

College of Arts and Science

SENIORS

Acklin, Robert, Memphis, Tenn.
Boyd, H. L., Beuna Vista, Tenn.
Bickers, H. A., Ripley, Tenn.
Brown, J. O., Lexington, Tenn.
Bruce, Grace, Sharon, Tenn.
Burns, Fred, Benton, Tenn.
Brasher, P. B., Jackson, Tenn.
Bodkin, L., Wyckliffe, Ky.
Castellaw, R. K., Maury City, Tenn.
Cole, C. H., Milan, Tenn.
Cope, Estelle, McMinnville, Tenn.
Carter, Mary, Bolivar, Tenn.
Collins, J. Floyd, Ozark, Ala.
Dance, J. C., Mayfield, Ky.
Drinkard, B. L., Trenton, Tenn.
Davis, C. E., Montezuma, Tenn.
Dexter, Miriam, Memphis, Tenn.
Dorris, Jewell, Bolivar, Tenn.
Etheridge, Fay, Jackson, Tenn.
Easley, Howard, Martin, Tenn.
Fulmer, M. M., Idabel, Okla.
Franks, Mrs. C. H., Jackson, Tenn.
Gilbert, Loreen, Jackson, Tenn.
Gilliam, Norris, Bells, Tenn.
Gooch, Lena, Selmer, Tenn.
Hargrove, B. L., Farmington, Ky.
Harris, T. T., Paducah, Ky.
Hudson, Print, Malesus, Tenn.
Hodge, James, McKenzie, Tenn.
Horn, I. N., Westport, Tenn.
Hall, B. F., Dyer, Tenn.
Huckaba, Carey, Huntingdon, Tenn.
Huey, H. T., Martin, Tenn.
Johnson, Horace, Jackson, Tenn.
Jones, Mrs. Linnie, Jackson, Tenn.
Jones, N. R., Memphis, Tenn.
Jackson, Virginia, Jackson, Tenn.
Jarvis, Elizabeth, Bells, Tenn.
Jamerson, L. W., Collierville, Tenn.
Keel, Paul, Woodburn, Ky.
Keele, F. D., Tullahoma, Tenn.
Koffman, I. H., Humboldt, Tenn.
Louis, Howard, Jackson, Tenn.
Lewis, Talmadge, Jackson, Tenn.
Lancaster, W. P., Eaton, Tenn.
McKendree, Eva, Arlington, Ky.
Muller, Mrs. A. C., Jackson, Tenn.
McMillon, Mrs. J. O., Collierville, Tenn.
Malone, George, Jackson, Tenn.
McKnight, Mary, Malesus, Tenn.
Nolen, Fannie Mai, Jackson, Tenn.
Newsom, R. Z., Winneboro, Texas.
Ozment, T. D., Halls, Tenn.
Pettigrew, W. R., Jackson, Tenn.
Patrick, Frances, Memphis, Tenn.
Polk, Clyde, Slidell, La.
Powers, Grace, Selmer, Tenn.
Pennington, J. A., Mercer, Tenn.
Pinkston, C. B., Adamsville, Tenn.
Pope, W. W., Jackson, Tenn.
Rutledge, Ray, Jackson, Tenn.
Rives, Oscar L., Jordan, Ky.
Rogers, Floyd, Huron, Tenn.
Rives, Mrs. O. L., Jordan, Ky.
Roberts, A. H., Key West, Fla.
Roland, C. P., Pocahontas, Tenn.
Stephenson, G. D., Finley, Tenn.
Strong, Annie, Cordova, Tenn.
Stallings, Edith, Halls, Tenn.
Smith, Simon, Bolivar, Tenn.
Stovall, J. Willis, Jackson, Tenn.
Smith, R. N., Jackson, Tenn.
Smith, Xena Lou, Amory, Miss.
Taylor, A. M., Rutherford, Tenn.
Tomerlyn, Lyle, Jackson, Tenn.
Todd, Alvin, Dickson, Tenn.
Waldrop, H. H., Idlewild, Tenn.
Witherington, A. M., Sharon, Tenn.
Wilson, W. E., Martin, Tenn.

JUNIORS

Allen, Webster, Pinson, Tenn.
Bryant, R. F., Franklin, N. C.
Ballard, Mary, Memphis, Tenn.
Beard, J. L., Arlington, Tenn.
Brewer, Jack, Bolivar, Tenn.
Cox, William, Jackson, Tenn.
Cox, Clara Rhea, Jackson, Tennessee.
Cox, Wayne, Troy, Tenn.
Carter, H. L., Jackson, Tenn.
Dixon, Raymond, Trenton, Tenn.
Frost, J. W., Wingo, Ky.
Hundley, Nelle, Mercer, Tenn.
Hudson, Harry, Malesus, Tenn.
Harris, Laverne, Whiteville, Tenn.
Harris, Pearl, Stanton, Tenn.
Hanner, W. S., Conway, Ark.
Jones, Harold S., Portland, Tenn.
Love, Hunter, Murray, Ky.
Lax, Joe, Hickory Valley, Tenn.
Lewis, Leasy, Jackson, Tenn.
Luper, M. E., Jacksonville, Texas.
Lanier, Mariana, Jackson, Tenn.
Murchison, H. C., Maury City, Tenn.
Meadows, Paul, Bradford, Tenn.
Mewborn, Mary K., Macon, Tenn.
Pinkerton, Lucille, Centerville, Tenn.
Pennington, Helen, Mercer, Tenn.
Phillips, Evelyn, Jackson, Tenn.
Robertson, W. C., Jacksonville, Tex.
Stone, Mary Lee, Union City, Tenn.
Skiles, Fern, Trenton, Tenn.

Stark, Lucy, Nashville, Tenn.
Spight, Sarah, Ripley, Miss.
Throgmorton, Dan, Wynnburg, Tenn.
Walker, Mary Sue, Jackson, Tenn.
Williams, O. O., Sheffield, Ala.
Watters, Lillian, Jackson, Tenn.
Waldrop, F. J., Idlewild, Tenn.
Young, Troy, Watertown, Tenn.

SOPHOMORES

Baxter, Clarence, Jackson, Tenn.
Burgess, Ollie Mae, Wingo, Ky.
Belew, Carl C., Bradford, Tenn.
Curlin, Ida, Brownsville, Tenn.
Curlin, Nina, Brownsville, Tenn.
Carter, Hal, Maury City, Tenn.
Davis, Lloyd, Chesterfield, Tenn.
Drewry, Ruth, Ripley, Miss.
Enochs, Frances, Jackson, Tenn.
Eckstein, Ellis, Trenton, Tenn.
Estes, Roy, Selmer, Tenn.
Froman, Belle, Memphis, Tenn.
Fulghum, Dorothy, Jackson, Tenn.
Franks, C. H., Jackson, Tenn.
Ferguson, Wm., Dyersburg, Tenn.
Green, J. F., Jackson, Tenn.
Gray, Clyde, Chalybeate, Miss.
Gilbert, Claire, Paris, Tenn.
Greer, Henry, Oakfield, Tenn.
Gleaves, Sadie, Jackson, Tenn.
Holland, J. J., Camden, Tenn.
Hargrove, Connie, Mayfield, Ky.
Hill, Robert, Baldwyn, Miss.
Hughes, Rex, Jackson, Tenn.
Jones, Glen, Portland, Tenn.
James, Justice, Murray, Ky.
Jones, Audrey, Trezevant, Tenn.
Kee, Malcolm, Bentonville, Ark.
Kinsey, Vern, Trenton, Tenn.
Kirkman, Bruce, Union City, Tenn.
Lambert, M. O., Bethel Springs, Tenn.
Little, Neal, Crutchfield, Ky.
Merriweather, Hewitt, Jackson, Tenn.
McMillon, J. O., Jackson, Tenn.
McMinn, Gladys, Trenton, Tenn.
Nance, Lila R., Ripley, Miss.
Pennington, Alvin, Halls, Tenn.
Polk, Vivian, Jackson, Tenn.
Ricketts, F. L., Jackson, Tenn.
Rudd, Russell, Fulton, Ky.
Spann, Liza, Murray, Ky.
Smith, Sue, Parsons, Tenn.
Skinner, Marie, Martin, Tenn.
Tuchfeld, Janice, Jackson, Tenn.
Walker, W. E., Sante Fe, Tenn.
Watters, Evelyn, Jackson, Tenn.
Woodson, Frank, Malesus, Tenn.

FRESHMEN

Alexander, Wray, McKenzie, Tenn.
Bramley, Norine, McLemoresville, Tenn.
Bramley, Thelma, McLemoresville, Tenn.
Baine, Helen, Henderson, Tenn.
Brooks, Warren, Bolivar, Tenn.
Bond, Elizabeth, Jackson, Tenn.
Boone, Ruth, Clinton, Ky.
Butler, Ina, Paris, Tenn.
Brown, Edwin, Bemis, Tenn.
Bishop, C. E., Memphis, Tenn.
Cole, Tennie B., Minor Hill, Tenn.
Counce, Lillian, Hamburg, Tenn.
Coleman, Clyde, McKenzie, Tenn.
Cooper, Charles A., Beuna Vista, Tenn.
Clifft, Warner, Whiteville, Tenn.
Carmack, George, Troy, Tenn.
Chambers, A. S., Booneville, Miss.
Charles, Edwin, Conway, Ark.
Davis, Kyle, Jackson, Tenn.
Dodds, C. L., Savannah, Tenn.
Darnall, W. L., Yuma, Tenn.
Deloach, Frank, Jackson, Tenn.
Etheridge, Bernis, Jackson, Tenn.
Evans, Grady, Liberty, Tenn.
Essary, Ernest, Lexington, Tenn.
Fletcher, Hollis, Dyer, Tenn.
Ford, Hester, Mercer, Tenn.
Farmer, Tom, Martin, Tenn.
Faris, Dwight, Jackson, Tenn.
Fowler, F. F., Somerville, Tenn.
Harris, Rayborne, Kenton, Tenn.
Hunt, Gladys, Gibson, Tenn.
Heaslet, Inez, Clinton, Ky.
Hicks, William, Jackson, Tenn.
Haskins, Robert, Hickman, Ky.
Hickman, Virgie, McLemoresville, Tenn.
Hicks, Mary, Jackson, Tenn.
Hinkle, Donald, Jackson, Tenn.
Harris, Mary, Whiteville, Tenn.
Hays, Eva, Moscow, Tenn.
Johnson, Robert, Jackson, Tenn.
Jarrett, Ben A., Westport, Tenn.
Kinsey, Ruby, Trenton, Tenn.
Keele, Lacy, Nashville, Tenn.
Lowe, Helen, Eagleville, Tenn.
Lowe, Cora Lynn, Eagleville, Tenn.
Latta, Robbie, Union City, Tenn.
Maness, Lorena, Henderson, Tenn.
Meeks, Chaille, Jackson, Tenn.
McClanahan, Carolyn, Jackson, Tenn.
Montgomery, Vernon, Lexington, Tenn.
Moore, H. B., Osceola, Ark.
Muse, Ruby, Wheeler, Miss.

Morelock, Constance, Jackson, Tenn.
Morelock, Eddie Ruth, Jackson, Tenn.
Morelock, W. S., Jackson, Tenn.
Prather, W. W., Selmer, Tenn.
Privett, Freeman, Alamo, Tenn.
Porter, Martha, Rutherford, Tenn.
Priddy, Hazel, Whiteville, Tenn.
Parker, Joe H., Jackson, Tenn.
Park, Ollie A., Union City, Tenn.
Rachel, Morris, Idabel, Okla.
Ray, Sarah, Carrolton, Miss.
Roy, Alpha, Abbeville, Miss.
Roy, Eunice, Abbeville, Miss.
Roy, Lyda, Abbeville, Miss.
Reesor, Verah, LaCenter, Ky.
Robinson, Clara, Selmer, Tenn.
Reed, Russell, Dyer, Tenn.
Rose, Virgil A., Brighton, Tenn.
Scott, Lucille, Lexington, Tenn.
Stewart, Roy, Greenville, Texas.
Speight, Neva, LaCenter, Ky.
Stone, Sallie J., Union City, Tenn.
Spight, Louise, Ripley, Tenn.
Sealand, B. D., Dyersburg, Tenn.
Self, Harold, Jackson, Tenn.
Strayhorn, J. W., Denmark, Tenn.
Siler, Lucy Mai, Jackson, Tenn.
Steen, Charley, Jackson, Tenn.
Stanfield, Catherine, Jackson, Tenn.
Short, Grace, Jackson, Tenn.
Thomason, Lyle, Westport, Tenn.
Travis, Margaret, Paris, Tenn.
Travis, Louise, Paris, Tenn.
Watters, Everett, Jackson, Tenn.
Williamson, Katherine, Fulton, Ky.
Walton, Ruth, Paris, Tenn.
Wicker, Otis, Waxahachie, Texas.
Wyatt, Ralph, Yorkville, Tenn.
Weaver, Louise, Jackson, Tenn.

SPECIAL AND UNCLASSIFIED

(Practically all of these have fully met college entrance requirements, and most of them are above Freshman grades).

Alexander, Melissa, Selmer, Tenn.
Anderson, Pauline, Henderson, Tenn.
Agnew, Minnie, Rutherford, Tenn.
Akin, Berta, Jonesville, Tenn.
Avent, Mag Ella, Malesus, Tenn.
Baldridge, P. B., Jackson, Tenn.
Brizendine, Lucille, Jackson, Tenn.
Barnes, Mrs. Ruth, Jackson, Tenn.
Barron, M. D., Trenton, Tenn.
Bishop, C. E., Bolivar, Tenn.
Blackmon, Love, Jackson, Tenn.
Barton, T. C., Greenfeild, Tenn.
Bradford, Mary, Jackson, Tenn.
Brigance, E. D., Henderson, Tenn.

Bartholomew, G., Yuma, Tenn.
Bodkin, Mrs. L., Halls, Tenn.
Blackmon, Josephine, Jackson, Tenn.
Boulton, J. W., Jackson, Tenn.
Carter, Miriam, McLemoresville, Tenn.
Canada, Pauline, Dyer, Tenn.
Cheatham, Maggie, Henderson, Tenn.
Chambers, Mrs. Essie, Ramer, Tenn.
Clark, Margaretta, Jackson, Tenn.
Chambers, S. R., Ramer, Tenn.
Caldwell, L. B., Jackson, Tenn.
Coleman, Doris, Henderson, Tenn.
Cobb, Carolyn, Union City, Tenn.
Cooper, Jesse, Dyer, Tenn.
Cowell, B. W., Camden, Tenn.
Davidson, Jim, Lexington, Tenn.
Davidson, Mrs. Annie, Henderson, Tenn.
Davis, Frances, Mercer, Tenn.
Davis, C. A., Millington, Tenn.
Darnall, W. L., Yuma, Tenn.
Davis, G. W., Guntown, Miss.
Doyle, Esther, Bolivar, Tenn.
Dunlap, Kittie, Humboldt, Tenn.
Dorris, Otis, Bolivar, Tenn.
Dorris, Elton, Bolivar, Tenn.
Davis, M. M., Jackson, Tenn.
Etheridge, Katie Lee, Bethel Springs, Tenn.
Evans, Camilla Mai, Trenton, Tenn.
Fisher, W. B., Dyer, Tenn.
Fulmer, Mrs. M. M., Idabel, Okla.
Fullerton, Rosaline, Benton, Mo.
Froman, Irline, Memphis, Tenn.
Gregory. Mary E., Jackson, Tenn.
Glisson, Anne, Rutherford, Tenn.
Glisson, Irma, Rutherford, Tenn.
Harris, Carrie L., Houlka, Miss.
Hanna, J. R., Hornsby, Tenn.
Halls, J. L., Halls, Tenn.
Haynes, Jane T., Trenton, Tenn.
Hicks, Hazel, Jackson, Tenn.
Haynes, J. B.
Hardeman, D. B., Henderson, Tenn.
Horton, Ross, Malesus, Tenn.
Harris, Robert, Humboldt, Tenn.
Hughes, Monta, Brighton, Tenn.
Huey, Mrs. H. T., Jackson, Tenn.
Hylton, Florence, Bolivar, Tenn.
Hunt, E. L., Fruitland, Tenn.
Johnson, W. C., Camden, Tenn.
Kinzie, Margaret, Jackson, Tenn.
Keller, Estelle, Toone, Tenn.
Knowles, J. W., Jackson, Tenn.
Koffman, Mary, Humboldt, Tenn.
Knight, C. L., Jackson, Tenn.
Knight, H. L., Jackson, Tenn.
Lea, T. D., Bells, Tenn.
Long, Zelma, Parsons, Tenn.

Lewis, Aaron, Jackson, Tenn.
Lake, Annie, Jackson, Tenn.
Langford, Elmer, Cookeville, Tenn.
Maness, Bonnie, Greenfield, Tenn.
Majors, C. L., Ramer, Tenn.
Main, Dorothy, Seneca, Mo.
McCaslin, A. B., Dyer, Tenn.
Morgan, M. L., Trenton, Tenn.
McMinn, R. E., Trenton, Tenn.
Michael, J. G., Booneville, Miss.
McElroy, S. L., Baldwyn, Miss.
Miles, Lottie, Martin, Tenn.
McLeary, Ila, Humboldt, Tenn.
Murray, Roger, Jackson, Tenn.
McCorkle, H. G., Martin, Tenn.
McFarland, Ruth, Twin Falls, Idaho.
Morrison, Kathleen, Martin, Tenn.
Morris, Chas. D., Kenton, Tenn.
Mount, Mrs. C. H., Booneville, Miss.
Moore, J. W., Bemis, Tenn.
Morgan, Ora Belle, Houlka, Miss.
McKissack, Frank, Denmark, Tenn.
Newberry, Curtis B., Gleason, Tenn.
Nelson, C. C., Garland, Texas.
Neville, Fred H., Bradford, Tenn.
Owens, Allie Mai, Dyer, Tenn.
Orr, Willis, Humboldt, Tenn.
Pannell, Joe
Penn, Joe, Fruitland, Tenn.
Pickler, Elah, Beuna Vista, Tenn.
Pickler, Connie, Jackson, Tenn.
Pressley, Pauline, Troy, Tenn.
Porter, A. B., Jackson, Tenn.
Price, Frances, Jackson, Tenn.
Patterson, Birdie, Humboldt, Tenn.
Penn, Jarrell, Humboldt, Tenn.
Powell, Lula May, Jackson, Tenn.
Phelan, Thettie, Trenton, Tenn.
Pryor, Annett, Mayfield, Ky.
Routon, Vera, Jackson, Tenn.
Robbins, Lillian, Jackson, Tenn.
Rogers, Lucille, Amory, Miss.
Rogers, Jessie B., Martin, Tenn.
Roland, O. D., Henderson, Tenn.
Roberts, J. W., Henderson, Tenn.
Robinson, W. N., Bolivar, Tenn.
Rhodes, C. E., Guntown, Miss.
Scruggs, Mary, Humboldt, Tenn.
Shepherd, Mary, Jackson, Tenn.
Short, J. E., Texarkana, Ark.
Shaw, Simeon, Mercer, Tenn.
Sheddan, Lyman F., Osceola, Ark.
Smith, W. F., West, Tenn.
Shearin, William, Hickory Valley, Tenn.
Sargent, S. S., Guntown, Miss.
Shaver, J. D., Jackson, Tenn.
Summett, Ewel, Henderson, Tenn.
Stayton, Tyman F., Jackson, Tenn.
Stratton, Everett, Jackson, Tenn.

Stovall, Mrs. J. W., Jackson, Tenn.
Savage, Julia, Ripley, Tenn.
Tipton, Lula, Dyersburg, Tenn.
Thompson, Nielman, Jackson, Tenn.
Thomas, Margaret, Bolivar, Tenn.
Todd, R. A., Trenton, Tenn.
Teague, Oda, Selmer, Tenn.
Warren, Leona, Jackson, Tenn.
Warren, H. E., Malesus, Tenn.
Wilson, Lloyd, Denmark, Tenn.
Wooten, Avery, Martin, Tenn.
Whitson, M. E., Trimble, Tenn.
Wilde, F. J., Jackson, Tenn.
Walters, Essie V.
West, J. L., Ridgely, Tenn.
Wilde, Lena, Jackson, Tenn.
Watson, Mary B.
Williams, Everett
Walker, H. J., Fruitland, Tenn.
Wooten, A. G., Selmer, Tenn.

VOCATIONAL STUDENTS

Alexander, Arthur M., Jackson, Tenn.
Arnold, Aubie Roy, Jackson, Tenn.
Barnes, William T., Henderson, Tenn.
Baker, Chas, A., Jackson, Tenn.
Belew, F. M., Jackson, Tenn.
Barrix, Stokey A., Jackson, Tenn.
Brown, Bill, Jackson, Tenn.
Cagle, Wm. P., Parker, Tenn.
Coleman, Geo. A., Lavinia, Tenn.
Deloach, Turner, Humboldt, Tenn.
Deming, Bedford, Jackson, Tenn.
Desmond, John T., Bradford, Tenn.
Fesmire, Robt. H., Juno, Tenn.
Fitzgerald, Robt. W., Jackson, Tenn.
Fisher, T. G., Jackson, Tenn.
Fuzzell, Ernest, Greenfield, Tenn.
Gaba, Martin F., Jackson, Tenn.
Hall, John L., Jackson, Tenn.
Houston, Noah A., Jackson, Tenn.
Johnson, Cletus H., Jackson, Tenn.
Jones, Hugh A., Jackson, Tenn.
Ivey, Roy H., Huron, Tenn.
Klutts, Henry, Gleason, Tenn.
Leopard, R. L., Jackson, Tenn.
Mathis, Lloyd, Jackson, Tenn.
Melton, Haven Lee, Jackson, Tenn.
Mullen, Wm. H., Toone, Tenn.
Murphy, J. R., Jackson, Tenn.
Newman, Perry T., Jackson, Tenn.
Raney, Norman, Jackson, Tenn.
Reid, Gilbert O., Jackson, Tenn.
Robbins, Herman H., Jackson, Tenn.
Savage, Roy C., Jackson, Tenn.
Stayton, C. H., Jackson, Tenn.
Tucker, Alfred W., Greenfield, Tenn.
Thweatt, Wm. T., Jackson, Tenn.

Thurmond, John F., Jackson, Tenn.
Vinson, Wm. S., Malesus, Tenn.
Walker, A. G., Jackson, Tenn.
Walker, Hubbard J., Fruitland, Tenn.
Warren, Hallard E., Malesus, Tenn.
Wheatley, Ernest L., Jackson, Tenn.
Wyatt, Bedford F., Jackson, Tenn.
  CORRESPONDENCE STUDENTS
Brigance, Mrs. E. D., Henderson, Tenn.
Edwards, E. H., Huntingdon, Tenn.
Floyd, C. L.

Freeman, E. L.
Gregory, Louise, Henning, Tenn.
Hope, Reverend, Humboldt, Tenn.
Johnson, C. C., Red Boiling Springs, Tenn.
Martin, Mrs. Laura, Grand Junction, Tenn.
McPeake, W. T., Lexington, Tenn.
Orr, E. L., Humboldt, Tenn.
Stacy, Minnie, Grand Junction, Tenn.
South, Alta, Poden, Miss.
Roland, C. P., Henderson, Tenn.
Roberts, Walter, Guntown, Miss.
Wyreeor, E.

College of Fine Arts

Piano

Atwood, Cora Mai
Ballard, Mary
Bryant, Bernice
Brooks, Mrs.
Buck, Helen
Clark, Margaretta
Clopton, Annie
Deaton, Willie
Gallimore, Florence
Harris, Pearl
Hawkins, Ramsey
Heaslet, Inez
Hurst, Wilma
James, Mary
Jernigan, Annie
Jernigan, H.
Jones, Glenn
Jones, N. R.
Mays, Mozell
McFarland, Ruth
Morgan, Maurine
Morgan, Walter
Morris, Minnie L.
Nance, Lila Ray
Phillips, Evelyn
Rozzell, Mary
Robbins, Mrs.
Stanfield, Catheryn
Smith, Mrs.
Stone, Sallie J.
Thomas, Mary
Turner, J.
Travis, Margaret
Walker, Emma Laura
Watters, Evelyn
Watters, Lillian
Young, Troy

Voice

Cox, Clara Rhea, Jackson, Tenn.
Carter, Miriam, McLemoresville, Tenn.

Franks C. H., Jackson, Tenn.
Gardner, Helen, Jackson, Tenn.
Gilliam, Norris, Bells, Tenn.
Hargrove, C. L., Mayfield, Ky.
Huckaba, C. J., Huntingdon, Tenn.
Hall, J. L., Jackson, Tenn.
Hicks, R. M., Hickman, Ky.
Jernigan, P. H.
Jones, Mrs., Jackson, Tenn.
Keele, Lacy, Nashville, Tenn.
Kinsey, Vern, Trenton, Tenn.
Knight, C. L., Jackson, Tenn.
Kinsey, Ruby, Trenton, Tenn.
Kinsey, Eulala, Trenton, Tenn.
Luper, M. E., Jacksonville, Texas.
Mays, Mozelle, Jackson, Tenn.
Powell, Lula, Jackson, Tenn.
Porter, Martha, Rutherford, Tenn.
Reesor, Verah, LaCenter, Ky.
Ricketts, F. L., Jackson, Tenn.
Strayhorn, J. W., Denmark, Tenn.
Short, J. E., Texarkana, Ark.
Throgmartin, Dan, Wynnburg, Tenn.
Walker, W. E., Santa Fe, Tenn.
Weiss, Evelyn, Jackson, Tenn.
Whaley, H. T., Charleston, N. C.
McFarland, Ruth, Humboldt, Tenn.
Buck, Helen, Jackson, Tenn.
Carter, Mrs., Jackson, Tenn.
Ogden, Mrs., Jackson, Tenn.
Prince, Mrs., Jackson, Tenn.
Vestal, M., Jackson, Tenn.
Walker, E. L., Jackson, Tenn.

Expression

Blackmon, Elizabeth
Campbell, E. C.
Cole, I. C.
Chamberlin, Grace
Castellaw, Mrs.
Drake, H. L.
Farress, Riley

Fitzgerald, R. W.
Gardner, Helen
Gray, Mrs. J. P.
Hargrove, C. L.
Hicks, R. M.
Johnson, Bradley
Jamerson, L. W.
James, Justice
Knight, C. L.
Levis, Aaron
Love, Hunter
McLeary, Ila
McKendree, E. F.
Moorefield, John
Muller, Alfredo
Murchison, H. C.
Nevill, Waldo

Pontius, Rita
Privett, Freeman
Pickler, Harold
Pickler, A. H.
Siler, Thomas
Short, J. E.
Sheddan, L. F.
Smith, Ned
Sealand, B. B.
Stamps, Frank
Todd, R. A.
Thomas, Martha
Whaley, H. T.
Waldrop, F. J.
Waldrop, H. H.
Watt, Mildred

Business College

Andrews, Stanley, Houlka, Miss.
Andews, King, Houlka, Miss.
Adkison, Gertrude, Union City, Tenn.
Blurton, R. L., Gadsden, Tenn.
Bolton, Pird, Bradford, Tenn.
Batchelor, Charles, Luray, Tenn.
Baker, Charles, Jackson, Tenn.
Berryhill, Clyde, McKenzie, Tenn.
Boyd, Lucy, Tiptonville, Tenn.
Baxter, C. W., Jackson, Tenn.
Bentley, Lamar, Whiteville, Tenn.
Bingham, John L., Kenton, Tenn.
Bell, Mary, Cornith, Miss.
Briggs, Blanche, Jackson, Tenn.
Bond, Sarah, Jackson, Tenn.
Blackwell, Mary, Jackson, Tenn.
Barton, Ralph, West Point, Miss.
Brown, Paul, Jackson, Tenn.
Barham, Mary, Jackson, Tenn.
Brown, Edwin, Bemis, Tenn.
Byars, Annie, Paris, Tenn.
Cofer, Ellen, Pinson, Tenn.
Coleman, George, Milan, Tenn.
Chalker, Glenn, Trimble, Tenn.
Crawford, Geo., Bardwell, Ky.
Coker, Obye, Trenton, Tenn.
Caldwell, Howard, Huntsville, Ala.
Chessor, Arthur, Trenton, Tenn.
Coppedge, LaVerne, Teague, Texas.
Corum, Louise, Union City, Tenn.
Coffey, Norma, Palestine, Ark.
Casey, Robert, Jackson, Tenn.
Carl, Wilkerson, Moscow, Ky.
Downing, R. G., LaVinia, Tenn.
Desmond, John T., Bradford, Tenn.
Dickinson, Roy, Denmark, Tenn.
Dickinson, Robert, Denmark, Tenn.

Duncan, Lissette, Columbus, Miss.
Eason, William, Brownsville, Tenn.
Everett, Vera, Hickman, Ky.
Edrington, Estelle, Jackson, Tenn.
Fry, Ernest, Jackson, Tenn.
Fenner, Florence, Jackson, Tenn.
Flake, Hessie, Wildersville, Tenn.
French, Marvin, Martin, Tenn.
Foster, Will H., Jackson, Tenn.
Froman, Irlnie, Memphis, Tenn.
Free, Nelle, Benton, Ky.
Grady, Florence, Humboldt, Tenn.
Garner, Annie Kate, Florence, Ala.
Gowan, Beatrice, Medina, Tenn.
Gobelet, Mrs. Goldie, Jackson, Tenn.
Glover, Hazel, Union City, Tenn.
Hurley, Otto, Corinth, Miss.
Haliburton, Ruby, Pinson, Tenn.
Holland, Roy, Medon, Tenn.
Holland, Lessie, Medon, Tenn.
Hemphill, C. R., Medina, Tenn.
Henley, Annie May, Jackson, Tenn.
Hudson, H. D., Brownsville, Tenn.
Hickey, Howard, Baldwyn, Miss.
Hurst, Willma, Parsons, Tenn.
House, Oscar, Whiteville, Tenn.
Hays, Lulu, Trenton, Tenn.
Hanna, Miriam, Ramer, Tenn.
Harrell, Alton, Cedar Grove, Tenn.
Henson, Earl, Luray, Tenn.
Horner, Vera, Trenton, Tenn.
Howlette, Lewis, Bemis, Tenn.
Hill, Johnsey J., Booneville, Miss.
Holmes, James A., Whiteville, Tenn.
Hammond, Lillie, Corinth, Miss.
Johnson, C. H., Milan, Tenn.
Johnson, Freelan, Fulton, Ky.
Jones, Geo. L., Milan, Tenn.

Jordan, Royal, Lexington, Tenn.
Jobe, Norman, Jackson, Tenn.
Justice, Bradford, Jackson, Tenn.
Jones, Sarah, Jackson, Tenn.
Kirk, Zelmer, Cedar Grove, Tenn.
Keller, William, Toone, Tenn.
Keating, Mrs. Ruth, Martin, Tenn.
Lewis, Dura, Westport, Tenn.
Lawson, Lessie, Oakland, Tenn.
Lowery, Ernie, Big Sandy, Tenn.
Lappin, Allie, Jackson, Tenn.
Langford, Paul, Alamo, Tenn.
Lay, Espie, Vildo, Tenn.
Leet, Mamie, Hickman, Ky.
Law, Sallie Lou, Trenton, Tenn.
Lasley, Lucille, Jackson, Tenn.
Leeper, Alice, Jackson, Tenn.
Mason, Ruth, Jackson, Tenn.
Melton, Haven, Jackson, Tenn.
McKinnon, J., Gates, Tenn.
Mebame, Lura, Kenton, Tenn.
Moore, Mayver, Denver.
Mulherron, Charles, Denmark, Tenn.
McCauley, Mary, Toone, Tenn.
McDougall, Ruth, Jackson, Tenn.
McClamrock, Chesley, Jackson, Tenn.
Moody, C. F., Paris, Tenn.
McIlwain, Mary D., Trenton, Tenn.
Meador, Earl, Elbridge, Tenn.
Murphy, Ralph, Jackson, Tenn.
Merriwether, Mayfield, Denmark, Tenn.
McLean, Margaret, Jackson, Tenn.
Mason, Hazel, Jackson, Tenn.
Moore, Brumley, Jackson, Tenn.
Mays, Leslie, Milan, Tenn.
Nicks, Pauline, Whistler, Tenn.
Norton, Ollie B., Jackson, Tenn.
Newman, P. T., Greenfield, Tenn.
Norman, Erline, Fulton, Ky.
Nanney, Tillman, Fulton, Ky.
Odenwald, Joseph, Jackson, Tenn.
Overton, C. H., Bells, Tenn.
Overton, Bessie, Greenfield, Tenn.
Osborne, Chas., Jackson, Tenn.
Outlaw, Almer, Medon, Tenn.
Palmer, Floyd, McKenzie, Tenn.
Pybass, Paul, Trenton, Tenn.
Phillips, W. T., Adamsville, Tenn.
Pegues, Blanche, Huntersville, Tenn.
Person, Ula, Jackson, Tenn.
Parker, Annie Mai, Jackson, Tenn.
Payne, Marie, Jackson, Tenn.
Perry, Mattie Maud, Trenton, Tenn.
Phillips, Harold, Elbridge, Tenn.
Parker, Delia, Whiteville, Tenn.
Peck, Dorothy, Jackson, Tenn.

Pitt, Homer, Humboldt, Tenn.
Rochelle, Arthur, Milan, Tenn.
Regan, Joe, Jackson, Tenn.
Reeves, Cloys, Greenfield, Tenn.
Rosser, Tom, Jackson, Tenn.
Roland, Obey, Woodland Mills, Tenn.
Ruscoe, Marion, Carrolton, Miss.
Robbins, Frank, Dyer, Tenn.
Robbins, Hortense, Piggott, Ark.
Reeves, D. Dale, Troy, Tenn.
Sammons, Elbert, Whiteville, Tenn.
Spencer, Walter, Medina, Tenn.
Smith, W. C., Milan, Tenn.
Snider, Guy, Trenton, Tenn.
Stark, Charles, Medina, Tenn.
Smith, R. N., Jackson, Tenn.
Swanner, Joe, Jackson, Tenn.
Simmons, Walter, Whiteville, Tenn.
Stayton, Clarence, Fulton, Ky.
Savage, Roy, Dyer, Tenn.
Sanford, Marshall, Elbridge, Tenn.
Speight, Fara, Paris, Tenn.
Stewart, Ruby, Lexington, Tenn.
Stuart, Charles E., Whiteville, Tenn.
Simerell, Robert, Elbridge, Tenn.
Spellings, Leon, Westport, Tenn.
Smith, Essie, Jackson, Tenn.
Swink, James, Monroe, La.
Stuart, Clifton, Whiteville, Tenn.
Thetford, Brown, Bradford, Tenn.
Turner, Mary Ella, Jackson, Tenn.
Teague, James, Luray, Tenn.
Teague, Joe, Toone, Tenn.
Taylor, I. O., Booneville, Miss.
Tillman, Manley, Jackson, Tenn.
Thompson, Bettye, Trenton, Tenn.
Turner, Mrs. C. A., Spartanburg, S. C.
Turner, C. A., Spartanburg, S. C.
Troutt, Margaret, Jackson, Tenn.
Thompson, Lala, Dyer, Tenn.
Tate, R. A., Water Valley, Miss.
Turner, Ralph, Dyer, Tenn.
Taylor, Bob, Trenton, Tenn.
White, Bennie, Lexington, Tenn.
Wyatt, B. F., Milan, Tenn.
White, Elizabeth, Jackson, Tenn.
Walker, A. G., Jackson, Tenn.
Webb, Virginia, Jackson, Tenn.
Williams, Jack, McKenzie, Tenn.
Walker, Paul, Paris, Tenn.
Wilkins, C. A., Henderson, Tenn.
Wilson, Gerthal, Big Sandy, Tenn.
Weiss, Talmage, Jackson, Tenn.
Wood, Pearle, Corinth, Miss.
Whitelaw, Vivian, Jackson, Tenn.
Westmoreland, Robt., Jackson, Tenn.

Yeates, Mrs. Ruth, Jackson, Tenn.
Young, Lessie, Greenfield, Tenn.
Young, Thelma, Jackson, Tenn.

TRAINING SCHOOL
Seniors

Barrix, S. A., Humboldt, Tenn.
Benge, Louise, Humboldt, Tenn.
Booth, Lela May, Jones, Tenn.
Cawthon, Elton, Beech Bluff, Tenn.
Cole, Ira, Trenton, Tenn.
Collins, Clara, Halls, Tenn.
Carlson, Clifford, Jackson, Tenn.
Campbell, C. R., Jackson, Tenn.
Deaton, Willie, Bethel Springs, Tenn.
Fitzgerald, Ware, Jackson, Tenn.
Gwaltney, Ernest, Dyersburg, Tenn.
Halford, Rachel, Jackson, Tenn.
Howard, M. B., Paducah, Ky.
Hendrix, Sudie, Fruitland, Tenn.
Morrison, R. E., Jackson, Tenn.
Morrison, Mrs. R. E., Jackson, Tenn.
Moore, John, Halls, Tenn.
Moore, Russell, Halls, Tenn.
Patterson, Russell, Trenton, Tenn.
Pratt, Millard, Trezevant, Tenn.
Rice, Marian, Jackson, Tenn.
Robbs, Hilda Mae, Jackson, Tenn.
Taylor, Allene, Greenfield, Tenn.
Williams, Maness, Selmer, Tenn.
Williams, Mildred, Jackson, Tenn.
Williams, Waldemar, Jackson, Tenn.

UNCLASSIFIED

Atwood, Cora Mae, Christiana, Tenn.
Black, Jerry, Jackson, Tenn.
Bennett, R. K., Fruitland, Tenn.
Baker, J. D., Jackson, Tenn.
Barnes, Wm. T., Henderson, Tenn.
Bishop, Hazel, Memphis, Tenn.
Boulton, J. D., Jackson, Tenn.
Collins, Ben, Lewisburg, Tenn.
Collie, Willie, Pinson, Tenn.
Couch, J. B., Jackson, Tenn.
Curlin, Mildred, Denmark, Tenn.
Clopton, Annie B., Nashville, Tenn.
Crews, Robbie, Paris, Tenn.
Dement, Mattie, Trenton, Tenn.
Day, Ruth, Jackson, Tenn.
Duke, Ola, Jackson, Tenn., R.F.D.
Faires, Riley, Guys, Tenn.
Fullerton, Rosaline, Benton, Mo.

Franks, Leon, Holladay, Tenn.
Gooch, Earl, Jackson, Tenn.
Griffin, Dorothy, Jackson, Tenn.
Gardner, Elizabeth, Jackson, Tenn.
Galyean, Lester, Corinth, Miss.
Gilmore, Buena, Dyer, Tenn.
Gallimore, Florence, Dresden, Tenn.
Halford, Rebecca, Jackson, Tenn.
Hargrove, Loreen, Farmington, Ky.
Hunt, Fanchion, Fruitland, Tenn.
Hall, John L., Jackson, Tenn.
Hammons, Parnell, Selmer, Tenn.
Hawkins, Ramsey, Jones, Tenn.
Herbert, Agnes E., Galt, Mo.
Howse, Charles, Jackson, Tenn.
Hurst, Arvey, Montezuma, Tenn.
Johnson, Jesse, Florence, Ala.
Juinger, Raymond L., Rockport, Ky.
Johnstone, Marion, Nashville, Tenn.
Jernigan, P. H., Lepanto, Ark.
Jones, Katie Joe, Jackson, Tenn.
Lake, Irene, Jackson, Tenn.
Lockman, Douglas, Hornsby, Tenn.
Moffitt, Lawrence, Jackson, Tenn.
McGill, Sarah, Yuma, Tenn.
Martin, Mrs. Laura, Chewalla, Tenn.
Mays, Mozelle, Jackson, Tenn.
McCoy, Martin, Memphis, Tenn.
Moore, Benton, Selmer, Tenn.
Moorefield, John, Clarksville, Tenn.
Morgan, C. L., Jackson, Tenn.
McAfee, Ernest, Dyersburg, Tenn.
Nevill, W. C., Jackson, Tenn.
Owen, Louise, Jackson, Tenn.
Patterson, Wendall, Jackson, Tenn.
Powell, Gladys, Jackson, Tenn.
Pettijohn, Catherine, Martin, Tenn.
Peck, Dorothy, Jackson, Tenn.
Rutledge, William, Jackson, Tenn.
Smith, John E. W., Ridgely, Tenn.
Smith, Ned, Medon, Tenn.
Stamps, F. H., Memphis, Tenn.
Siler, Thomas, Silerton, Tenn.
Taylor, Robert, Eaton, Tenn.
Turner, H. A., Jackson, Tenn.
Tiffany, Russell, Jackson, Tenn.
Weaver, Elizabeth, Jackson, Tenn.
Weaver, Earl, Jackson, Tenn.
Wood, Curtis, Jackson, Tenn.
Weiss, Evelyn, Jackson, Tenn.
Whaley, H. T., Charleston, S. C.
Wright, Givens, Nashville, Tenn.

Teachers
(Summer School)

Akin, Thomas R.
Anderson, Erline, Medina, Tenn.

Arnold, Lucille, Kenton, Tenn.
Arnold, Nannie, Pinson, Tenn.

Atkins, Annie, Henry, Tenn.
Atkins, Mrs. R. V., Bradford, Tenn.
Birdwell, Mrs. B. C., Yuma, Tenn.
Birdwell, Era, Buena Vista, Tenn.
Bell, Elsie May, Springville, Tenn.
Buford, Minnie May, Friendship, Tenn.
Booth, Annie May, Guntown, Miss.
Boren, Myra, Oakfield, Tenn.
Barnwell, Mrs. Hazel, Medina, Tenn.
Bryant, Mrs. Ruth, Bolivar, Tenn.
Bond, Sarah, Jackson, Tenn.
Bennett, Lela, Alamo, Tenn.
Byrd, Daisy, McNairy, Tenn.
Barber, Madge, Bethel Springs, Tenn.
Bailey, Elizabeth, Mercer, Tenn.
Bright, Nannie Lou, Chalybeate, Miss.
Batchelor, Grace, Trenton, Tenn.
Boulton, Mattie, Cades, Tenn.
Boyd, Mary, Buena Vista, Tenn.
Byrum, Thelma, Jones, Tenn.
Boswell, Lottie, Medina, Tenn.
Bowman, Mrs. W. C.
Brown, Esther, Beacon, Tenn.
Brasher, Ruth, Beech Bluff, Tenn.
Brasher, Lucille, Scott's Hill, Tenn.
Boyette, Johnnie Lou, Rutherford, Tenn.
Curlin, Prencess, Brownsville, Tenn.
Crawford, Mrs. I.
Comer, Evie, Denmark, Tenn.
Compton, Anna, Henderson, Tenn.
Compton, Mrs. Mattie
Carter, Minelle, Jackson, Tenn.
Cobb, Nannie Bell, Jackson, Tenn.
Crabtree, Mrs. W. F., Henderson, Tenn.
Cobb, John P., Bethel Springs, Tenn.
Cox, Mrs. Mattie, Ridgely, Tenn.
Crowe, Gilcie, Adamsville, Tenn.
Cloare, Trilla, Dyer, Tenn.
Critenden, Frances, Jackson, Tenn.
Crittenden, Emma, Jackson, Tenn.
Canada, Pauline, Dyer, Tenn.
Crowe, Mattie, Adamsville, Tenn.
Carter, Bernice, Maury City, Tenn.
Dozier, Martha, Kenton, Tenn.
Durrett, Elizabeth, Bolivar, Tenn.
Davidson, Roxie, Dyer, Tenn.
Darnall, Ollie B., Yuma, Tenn.
Dougan, Eva, Bells, Tenn.
Dodds, Mrs. Inez, Friendship, Tenn.
Duck, Edgar Lee, Dyer, Tenn.
Deen, Lucille, Whiteville, Tenn.
Dement, Lena Mai, Dyer, Tenn.
Davis, Enoch, Guntown, Miss.
Davenport, Bethel, Medina, Tenn.

Davidson, Lillous, Medina, Tenn.
Davis, Angie, Pinson, Tenn.
Eason, Janie M., Jackson, Tenn.
Ellis, Irma, Newbern, Tenn.
Eaton, Pink, Henderson, Tenn.
Eason, S. L., Bethel Springs, Tenn.
Ezzell, Sallie B., McKenzie, Tenn.
Eason, Louise, Brownsville, Tenn.
Eason, Mrs. Mattie, Henderson, Tenn.
Forsythe, Louise, Humboldt, Tenn.
Forsythe, Eva, Humboldt, Tenn.
Fisher, Mrs. Lida, West, Tenn.
Fisher, Ollie, Dyer, Tenn.
Follis, Mary, Trenton, Tenn.
Farris, Orpha, Adamsville, Tenn.
Gwynne, Henry N., Williston, Tenn.
Gilbert, Mabel
Gilbert, Willie May, Jackson, Tenn.
Gilbert, J. C., Jackson, Tenn.
Griggs, Sara
Gunter, Mrs. W. I.
Gregory, Grace, Memphis, Tenn.
Gunter, Grace, Jackson, Tenn.
Graham, E. Morris, Corinth, Miss.
Glisson, Mai, Huntingdon, Tenn.
Gilkey, Ruth, McKenzie, Tenn.
Gunter, Ellen
Glibert, Maude, Jackson, Tenn.
Gilley, Jennie Lou, Jackson, Tenn.
Gullett, Maude, Camden, Tenn.
Gullett, Mabel, Camden, Tenn.
Holly, H. T.
Hocking, Nita
Hillhouse, Bethel, Bolivar, Tenn.
Haynes, Mrs. J. T., Medon, Tenn.
Hays, J. B., Cades, Tenn.
Hart, Lucille, Lexington, Tenn.
Hallowell, Ada, Westport, Tenn.
Halliburton, M., Rutherford, Tenn.
Howard, Martha, Jackson, Tenn.
Hanna, Miriam, Ramer, Tenn.
Hawk, Allie, Jackson, Tenn.
Hundley, Eddie Mai, Jackson, Tenn.
Hamilton, Mary D., Humboldt, Tenn.
Haynes, Carrie C., Pinson, Tenn.
Holt, Mrs. Otha, Milan, Tenn.
Haynes, Lela Mae, Pinson, Tenn.
Holmes, Alberta, Lexington, Tenn.
Halter, Ida, Darden, Tenn.
Ivey, Frances, Jackson, Tenn.
Jacobs, Eloise, Bolivar, Tenn.
Jones, Bessie, Jackson, Tenn.
Johnson, Thelma, Ridgely, Tenn.
Jones, Ada, Pinson, Tenn.
Jones, Lurline, Bells, Tenn.
Jones, Mary, Trenton, Tenn.
Jones, Eura, Trenton, Tenn.
Jones, Mrs. R. B.
Johnson, F. L., Pinson, Tenn.

Johnson, Mrs. F. L., Pinson, Tenn.
Johnson, Mrs. Ernest L., Beech Bluff, Tenn.
Kane, Corenna, Jackson, Tenn.
Kendrick, Mary, Jackson, Tenn.
Koffman, Katheryn, Trenton, Tenn.
Koenig, Iness, Jackson, Tenn.
Luckey, Ruby, Humboldt, Tenn.
Law, Blondell, Trenton, Tenn.
Luckey, Sue, Humboldt, Tenn.
Louis, Caroline
Lindsey, Erby, Darden, Tenn.
Laughter, Eunice, Memphis, Tenn.
Latham, Katy Lou, Pinson, Tenn.
Lambert, Maryck, Bolivar, Tenn.
Lambert, Willie M., Bolivar, Tenn.
Littlefield, Edna, Adamsville, Tenn.
Morgan, Maurine
Morgan, Ora Bell, Houlka, Miss.
McKinney, Mrs. Booker, Jackson, Tenn.
Moore, Lala Mai, Pinson, Tenn.
McCauley, Mary, Toone, Tenn.
Martin, Ethel, Jackson, Tenn.
Maxwell, Mrs. Calla, Darden, Tenn.
McIlwain, Emma Lou, Parsons, Tenn.
McAuley, Charline, Jackson, Tenn.
Mitchell, Marguerite, Dyer, Tenn.
McKinley, Josephine, Fruitland, Tenn.
Maness, Clyde, Henderson, Tenn.
Morgan, Katie Lou, Montezuma, Tenn.
Miller, Mary, Denmark, Tenn.
Moore, Bernice, Whiteville, Tenn.
Mtichell, Maude, McLemoresville, Tenn.
McNeely, Ella, Kenton, Tenn.
Nord, Mildred, Jackson, Tenn.
Neal, Mary, Henry, Tenn.
Neal, Laurale, Henry, Tenn.
Naylor, Mary, Henderson, Tenn.
Nicholson, Onieda, Whiteville, Tenn.
Nelson, Loraine
O'Neal, Zelma, Scott's Hill, Tenn.
O'Neal, Mabel, Jackson, Tenn.
Outlaw, Ousey, Medon, Tenn.
Orr, Vashti, Wildersville, Tenn.
Page, Vernelle, Trenton, Tenn.
Pettigrew, Ludie, Westport, Tenn.
Poston, Willie Lee
Parham, Dewey James, Saltillo, Miss.
Peters, Etheline, Pinson, Tenn.
Pegues, Elizabeth, Jackson, Tenn.
Perrv. Aurelle, Greenfield, Tenn.
Pruett, Mrs. Herbert
Pond, Ruth, Jackson, Tenn.
Pinkston, Lela T., Bells, Tenn.

Raney, Norman
Robbins, Mrs. Irene, Henderson, Tenn.
Roberts, Georgie, Henderson, Tenn.
Roberts, Flora, Henderson, Tenn.
Reeves, Cozie, Trenton, Tenn.
Rhea, Lucille, Jackson, Tenn.
Ray, Bertha, Walnut, Miss.
Roundtree, Belle, Beech Bluff, Tenn.
Richardson, Christine, Jackson, Tenn.
Reams, Vera Ann, Humboldt, Tenn.
Reed, Ruby, Beech Bluff, Tenn.
Rucker, Mrs. Linnie
Saine, Fay, Dyer, Tenn.
Smith, Lucy, Bolivar, Tenn.
Shearin, Annie, Bolivar, Tenn.
Summers, J. W., Shannon, Miss.
Summers, Mrs. J. W., Shannon, Miss.
Simpson, Leroy E., Shaw, Miss.
Smith, Clarice, Jackson, Tenn.
Smith, A. E., Bolivar, Tenn.
Smith, Hildreth, Kenton, Tenn.
Stewart, Georgia Mai, Athens, Ala.
Smith, Maggie, Ridgely, Tenn.
Smith, Vera, West, Tenn.
Smith, Vera May, Springville, Tenn.
Still, Mary E., Jackson, Tenn.
Smith, Mrs. Burcie, Reagan, Tenn.
Siler, Naomi, Silerton, Tenn.
Smith, Lydia, Friendship, Tenn.
Simpson, Mrs. W. B., Friendship, Tenn.
Thomas, L. L., Dyer, Tenn.
Tatum, John, Jackson, Tenn.
Thompson, Mattie Green, Jackson, Tenn.
Turner, Clara, Middleton, Tenn.
Thompson, Cecil, Dyer, Tenn.
Thorne, Mrs. Dora, Denmark, Tenn.
Thomas, Mae, Jackson, Tenn.
Taylor, Ruby, Jackson, Tenn.
Todd, B. A., Beacon, Tenn.
Tyson, Mrs. J. A., Denmark, Tenn.
Tisdale, Lucille, Whiteville, Tenn.
Taylor, Rossie, Pocahontas, Tenn.
Taylor, Allie Belle, Bradford, Tenn.
Weeks, Pearl, Henderson, Tenn.
Williams, Rose C., Jackson, Tenn.
Valentine, Thelma, Denmark, Tenn.
Vincent, Gladys, Dyer, Tenn.
Wheat, Hallie, Jackson, Tenn.
Wilson, Allie
Wilson, Annie, Lexington, Tenn.
Willoughby, Trixie, Jackson, Tenn.
Wilson, Cora May, Lexington, Tenn.
Whaley, Martha, Middleton, Tenn.
Watlington, Lucille, Pinson, Tenn.
Williams, Freda, Juno, Tenn.

Wright, Terry, Lexington, Tenn.   Wilson, Loraine, Mercer, Tenn.
Walker, Noraine, Chesterfield, Tenn.

SUMMARY OF GRADUATES

College of Arts and Sciences

Bachelor of Arts Degree..45
Bachelor of Science Degree..14
Bachelor of Music Degree 2
                                                                    —
            Total Degrees   61
Normal Diploma 11
Home Economics Diploma 5
Diploma in Music 4
Post-Graduate in Music 1
Home Economics Certificate 3
Certificate in Music 3

            Total   27

Total Certificates of Graduation from the College.............   88
Graduates from the Training School   26

            Total Graduates   114

SUMMARY OF ENROLLMENT

College

Seniors 79
Juniors 39
Sophomores 47
Freshmen 92
Unclassified 157

                                                         414   414

Specials

Vocational 43
Correspondence 15
Piano 37
Voice 37
Expression 40

                                                         172   172

            Total College   586

College of Arts and Sciences

Training School   96
Business College   194
Teachers (Summer School)   228

                                                                   1106
Less Duplicates   90

                                                                   1016

A Great Memorial

We suggest a great and worthy memorial for someone as follows: A dormitory for girls equipped for the clubbing or light housekeeping plan that has been so successfully in progress here for the last seven years. We have had 300 girls in the history of the club to take advantage of this special boarding plan, and they are all enthusiastic over it. It has enabled many to get an education who could not otherwise have done so. They have reduced the cash cost of their board to an average of $10 a month. We need a large building properly planned and equipped to take care of 100 girls. We suggest that the net rents from the building be turned over to a loan fund and be lent out as other funds. This fund would grow under the annual rents and compound interest through the years so that within a century would amount to more than $13,000,000. Other buildings might be erected before the close of that period and thus hundreds of thousands of girls be helped through school. The imagination is staggered at what it would do in the next century—and yet universities stand for a thousand years. This is a great suggestion to somebody.

Rules and Regulations

The above funds, except those specially designated otherwise, are let out under the following regulations: First, funds are available to students who have demonstrated their real worth in school. Class records and deportment in general are considered. They must be recommended by all of their teachers. Second, six per cent interest is charged. Third, at present, owing to the limited amount at our disposal, we must limit the amount loaned any student to one hundred dollars a year. Fourth, students who do not have insurance protection or property must offer approved security.

Form of Will

I, _____, hereby will and bequeath to Union University _____ to be used as follows:_____

Signed_____

Place and Date_____

Witness_____

(See page 32)

Lightning Source UK Ltd.
Milton Keynes UK
UKHW020308261118
332889UK00007B/241/P